The Book of the Nine-Tailed Fox

A Handbook of Chinese Witchcraft and Alchemy in the Fox Tradition

By Jason Read

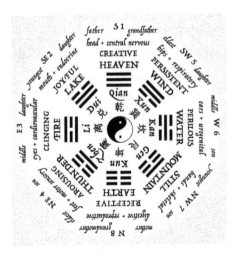

The methodologies in this book stem from the author's own experiences. The Reader must not regard the information as an alternative to medical advice, which he should obtain from a qualified professional. The Reader who thinks he might be suffering from a medical condition should seek medical advice immediately. The Reader who is already in receipt of medical treatment should not discontinue or delay this treatment or disregard medical advice as a consequence of having read the information in this book. The author and the publishers cannot accept legal responsibility for any problem arising out of experimenting with the methods described.

Fox Magic

The Book of the Nine-Tailed Fox

A Handbook of Chinese Witchcraft and Alchemy in the Fox Tradition

By Jason Read

Dedicated to my soulmate
and Priestess of Hu Xian, Vicky Yun

Contents

Acknowledgements

I would like to thank the following people for their indispensable help and support in completing this volume:

My true love and confidante and priestess in Dao, Vicky Yun for her aid and suggestions in translating some of the more obscure Chinese terms.

Kozou Shugiyama, priest and monk of the Shingon and Mikkyo traditions and one of the few with the lore of Onmyodo under his obi (belt).

My teacher and Master Dr. Liang, an amazing and humble powerhouse of Asian occult knowledge.

To my ever patient and wonderful editor Mogg Morgan who made wonderful suggestions and took the risk to publish this series of Chinese sorcerous texts. Adesh Adesh.

The Chinese Magick Series

The mysteries of Chinese occultism have long been hidden from the West, largely due to the cultural and language barriers between us. Also because of the reluctance of the Chinese Masters to part with their knowledge.

For this reason we are producing this series of books to fill that gap in the knowledge of most western magicians. This knowledge comes from both oral and written sources that can only be found in Chinese communities. The author has travelled extensively in China and Malaysia and personally learned under several teachers from a school of practical magic known as Maoshan.

Maoshan is a school of magic dealing with the interaction of the seen and unseen worlds, with a knowledge base dating back thousands of years to the time of the ancient shaman kings who ruled that area of China known as the Sichuan Plateau. Over many generations the Maoshan school developed hundreds if not thousands of unique techniques to alleviate the challenges of life as well as to explore our spiritual nature and that of the cosmos.

Maoshan, the school devoted to practical magic is unveiled in these books for the first time in the English language. We hope this opens a door to the mysterious world of the ancient chinese sorcerers. Forthcoming volumes include:

Thunder Magic.
Secrets of Chinese necromancy.
Chinese love and sex magic and alchemy
Mysteries of Chinese Star magick.
Chinese talismanic Magick.
The Book of the Nine Tailed Fox. (this volume)

Chinese Magickal Healing and Rejuvenation.
Chinese Magick of Fortune and Gambling.
The Training of a Chinese Sorcerer.
Chinese Magical Defence and Attack.

Introduction

This may be a topic wholly new to the average western reader though it will have familiar elements, after all, all true Mysteries in the true sense of the word have a common thread.

Some readers may be familiar with the Lady Fox from various pop-cultural references in Japanese anime or Hong Kong movies and even video games. It is Kitsune, the fox spirit of the west that is most accessible to the average western audience.

However the cultus of the Fox goes far further back than her appearance in Japan and Korea, her roots seemingly going as far back as the ancient tantric mysteries of India.

I am a practitioner in the magical tradition of Taoism and it was in China that I learned the basics of the Fox Fairy as she is sometimes called. However China is a very conservative country and it seems obvious to me that a lot was implied but never spoken of, or perhaps even forgotten.

I ventured into the depths of the mysteries of the Fox Lady and the path took me in many directions and through many synchronicities on that journey.

While I preserve the fox tradition as passed to me, I do add some further material, also based on traditions that connect with her 'sadhana' [glossary]. I expect there will be an outcry from some Taoist and Shingon purists since in a sense I am resurrecting the heterodox Shingon cult of the Tachikawa. The logic of this decision will become clear. I am certain this is the correct move.

In this way, we rise above the apparent shallowness of the Fox Temple as seen in contemporary Hong Kong for example, where the Fox Fairy has merely become a means to become a more attractive person in the world of film and music.

In this book, I am giving the keys to true gnosis of the Path of the Nine-Tailed Fox.

Please enjoy and above all, practice.

Jason Read
Southampton, UK
September 2021

Hu Li Jing
The Fox Spirit In Legend

A good starting place in examining the fox legend is the storytelling tradition. Stories, myths and legends are often preservers of a certain kind of folk wisdom and will allow us to immerse ourselves in the seemingly exotic world of the Hu Li Jing or the Fox Spirit.

1. The Tale Of Mr. Sun

A certain elderly gentleman named Mr Sun after a long day decided to take a short nap. As he lay down, for a brief moment he thought he saw from corner of his eye, something climb up onto his bed. Suddenly he felt a strange sensation as if he was floating in the clouds, almost as if he was being carried up into the air. He instinctively knew that this was a case of fox possession. Opening his eyes ever so slightly he saw the fox spirit. It had yellow fur and a viridian mouth, quietly and sneakingly wriggling up from the end of the bed. As it reached his feet he felt his legs become paralysed. However, as soon as it reached his abdomen he quickly sat up in bed and seized the fox tightly in his strong grip and cried out to his wife. His wife brought him a sash and tied the fox up. The fox tried to escape by changing size. One moment as thin as a bamboo stem and next bloated like a large pot. His wife meanwhile had returned with a knife to kill the fox. Having got the knife the man turned round to stab the fox, but it had vanished. There was nothing but an empty loop in the sash.

2. The Tale Of Gong Xueli

There once lived a man who was the descendant of Confucius, named Gong Xueli. An accomplished poet and scholar, he went to see his friend in Tiantai. On arrival, he found his friend had died so he stayed overnight at a local temple.

Journeying further he found himself caught in a terrible blizzard, but luckily he found refuge at the home of a well to do family. He knocked on the door and a young gentleman opened the door. It soon transpired that the young man was named Huangfu and that he and his family were temporarily borrowing the house from the great Shan family. Soon enough, learning of Gong's plight, Huangfu agreed to employ him as a tutor.

The family treated him very well, the father visited and happily gave him fine clothes. Huangfu was an excellent student. One day a girl named Fragrance played the zither in an unusually lively style. Gong was struck by her beauty and grace. Huangfu however noted that there were greater beauties to behold.

Huangfu was an extremely excellent student, but one day Gong woke up extremely sick. Huangfu was very worried and seemed to call someone.

Then walked in two of the most beautiful girls Gong had ever seen. One named Grace and one named Pine. They were the sisters of Huangfu. Both were as supple and as lithe as fresh willow, with a sparkle in their eyes.

Grace took Gong's pulse and immediately declared that his heart meridian was affected and also discovered a swelling on his body ... She took off a golden bracelet and pressed the swelling and immediately it lessened. She cut a slit in the pustule and drained the dark blood. Then, from her mouth appeared a red pill which she pressed onto the wound. She retrieved it and swallowed it again. He was cured.

Soon enough love was in the air, and ultimately he fell in love with Pine. In due time they were married.

One day however, Huangfu appeared to him and said they must go because the Shan family was ready to return to the house.

With that Huangfu disappeared. Pine was not only beautiful and loyal but remained with him and bore him a son.

Some years later Grace visited Gong and Pine. She admitted they really are of the fox folk and that he had married the race of fox and humanity together. She related to him that her fox family were in danger.

Gong agreed to defend them. He was standing guard outside their door when there was a tremendous thunderstorm. Suddenly the earth opened up and a terrible monster with a bird-like beak and claws emerged holding Grace. He leapt forward and upward with his sword. There was a crash of thunder. The creature let Grace go but Gong was dead. The two sisters carried Gong into the house and opened his mouth with a golden hairpin. Grace seemingly kissed Gong, but she was really pushing the red pill of mysterious medicine into his body. Thus he lived again.

3. A Bottle And A Fox

There was once a woman greatly afflicted, being possessed by a fox. However, whenever her husband came home, the fox spirit would leap into a bottle.

One day as soon as the fox leapt into the bottle she grabbed it, plugged it up with cotton and began boiling it. She heard screams for mercy coming from the bottle. Finally, when she opened it, she saw a mix of fur and blood.

4. The Spell Of The Fox

There was once a great physician named Dong Xiasi. One day he returned home somewhat inebriated and saw, with some alarm, that his bedroom door was ajar.

Opening it he saw one of the most beautiful women he had ever seen, lying there on his bed asleep. He went to the bed and passing his hand under the cover began to caress the contours of her lithe body. The skin was soft and in his fervour, he let his hands pass down to her lower regions passing over the curve of her lower back and her shapely rear. Suddenly he bumped into something strange. It was a bushy fox's tail! In horror, he drew back, when all of a sudden the girl grasped his wrist.

"Don't kill me Miss Fairy" he cried. The girl feigned shock and surprise. "What is it about my body that makes you think this thing dear sir?" she said.

"Well, I felt your tail of course".

She giggled almost coquettishly, "Of course, I haven't got a tail, I just think you have been at the wine and the hour is late."

She grabbed his hand and let it pass over her body again. Indeed this time there was no tail.

Not being able to resist the sheer eroticism of the girl he soon found himself plunging into her well. As the month went by and her visits to his bed increased, Dong began to visibly waste away. He grew thin and haggard. He was forced to see a physician who told him frankly that he was bewitched.

Even when he resisted the fox maiden, the dreams of her were so intense that he ejaculated and soon he was coughing up blood. Soon after this Dong died.

The Fox Maiden turned her attention to his friend, a certain Mr Wang. He slept with her and also began having strange erotic dreams about the beautiful ethereal girl. Soon, he too began to waste away and become haggard. However, his wife noticed and warned him that his new mistress was in fact a fox and that she being a Yin spirit was extracting his Yang essence to lengthen her life, increase her magic and beauty. She advised him to burn some sandalwood.

That night when the fox maiden entered the bedroom smelling the incense she was immediately disturbed and began to complain.

Such stories about the fox give us an insight into their ambiguity and in a sense their neutrality.

On the one hand, the fox spirit is a beautiful maiden or wise man who can heal, bring fortune and blessings ... even discoursing on the Tao and teaching alchemy and magic. On the other hand, they can be deadly and in their Yin capacity drain the Yang essence from a man until he is a husk and passes into the next world, while she remains young and beautiful. The Huli jing can be both a teacher and loyal wife who can even bring forth children, or a succubus or a vampire with a wicked nature.

It is this ambiguity that earmarks the Fox Spirit as a creature of the liminal ... of the in-between, at the crossroads of nature. Neither goddess nor demon, neither human nor entirely spirit, the fox exists at the crossroads, at the veil between worlds and that is her power.

It is also the power that we access when we commune with her, in at least one way we meet her at the meeting point between sleep and dream, at the in-between times of consciousness and the dream state.

The stories above reflect the dual nature of the fox spirit. She can prey on the living and even possess them or she can love them and bring wealth, love and prosperity.

The cultus of the Fox is indeed Yin in nature and it has its dangers. Yin is dark and associated not only with the power of the receptive feminine but with the idea of the ghostly world of death as we shall see. It has its own glamour to bewitch and enchant and even catch our soul so we are oblivious to the dangers that lurk in the black depths of Yin. Yet the Yin world is what completes cosmic manifestation, Without Yin and Yang working together there can be no existence.

I cannot help but draw a parallel to the European idea of the Faerie. The reader should now cast from their mind the modern idea of the fairy developed in Victorian England. They were once considered a powerful race existing in the twilight realms. Robert Kirk described them as the secret Commonwealth. These faerie folk were a race living in the twilight realms between our world and the unseen world, so they were often associated with in-between times and places such as the dusk, or the Summer Solstice for example. They were beautiful and skilled in the magical arts and yet could equally curse you and blight your life. The faeries were often associated with witchcraft and even appeared at Sabbats instructing her followers in the ways of the dark arts. They have a strongly ethereal beauty. Indeed the word glamour itself appears to have come from the enchantment faeries could cast on a mortal's perception.

Just as Fox Spirits could possess the bodies of human beings and either dispense wisdom or drive a person to insanity, or dragging their soul to Elphame (away with the faeries), so in Taoist and Chinese folk belief, the fox could possess a person and live through them causing havoc and fear in the community. There is even an element of lycanthropy to this phenomenon as we shall see.

The Fox Spirit and the western faerie seem to be of the same ilk. Beings of the twilight, magical, dual in nature and somehow connected with eroticism and death. Yes, for faeries were often said to live among the ancient tombs and some scholars connect them with early practices of ancestor worship.

A rather charming translation of fox is as Fox Fairy, and because of the parallels I drew above I am settling on this transliteration. Very commonly she is known as HU XIAN.

Hu means fox. Xian is a little more complex. Xian essentially means one who has cultivated through special practices such as alchemy, meditation and magic a certain kind of exalted immortal transcendence. This state of being Xian is the ultimate goal of practical Tao and is similar in idea, but not exactly to becoming a Buddha or a Master.

The fox is indeed a kind of spirit that is cultivated to reach certain goals. Yet the word Fairy suits her aptly.

Fox spirits are not only female, though that is the most common manifestation. There are also tales of handsome fox men and even fox uncles with long white beards dispensing the wisdom of the ages.

The Huxian of the Fox Society to which I belong however is female, we shall examine more closely later why this is so.

Dark Foxes

As implied, not all foxes are a positive force in this world. On the most minor level, fox spirits can invade our bodies and use us. They can appear as vampiric glamorous entities and drain the pearly essence of a man to promote their magical development at the expense of his life. They can be tricksters and sometimes downright evil.

Many tales of the Fox spirit reveal a vampiric nature, specifically that of Yang energy and particularly of males i.e. the sexual energies. Yet even this in itself is an avenue of magical technique and gnosis to the discerning magician. Some Foxes, therefore, are not the friend of mankind and bring with them great danger and destruction.

One story concerns a certain Guan Yin temple somewhere in China. Guan Yin, for those who don't know, is a bodhisattva of the Buddhist tradition mostly seen as a beautiful maiden dressed in white clothes. A western equivalent would be St. Mary in both form and function. However, the main statue of the Goddess somehow became the seat of a crafty female fox spirit who fed off the energies of the participants as well as enjoying the offerings set before her. The people of this particular temple became weaker and sickened, and many experienced terrible dreams, a characteristic of a psychic attack.

The head priestess of this same temple began to have trouble in one of her eyes. Red and weeping, her eye became constantly a source of pain and marred the beauty of the priestess.

Concerned, one of the congregation called in a local fangshi wizard. At once, with his clairvoyant sight, he saw forms of white foxes wrapped around the auras of the people. They had not been devoting themselves to the blessed Guanyin but rather a Fox spirit who in her escape from some other chaos she had caused had been injured in one eye. Hence the priestess, who was undoubtedly the focus of the wily fox spirit's actions had developed a physical expression of that fox's energetic injury.

Chinese and Japanese occult history point to a few tales where powerful foxes have become great influencers in a negative manner throughout history.

There are two particularly famous tales that seem to be a continuation of one concerning the ancient fox spirit.

The story begins at the end of the Shang Dynasty. At this time there was a great and mighty Emperor named Zhou (1025-1046 BCE). By all accounts, he was, at first, a wise and sharp-minded Emperor. He deeply cared for the people of his Empire and was heavily involved in state policies.

One day, however, sitting in court there appeared the most beautiful and graceful woman he had ever seen. Tall with long graceful limbs, hair as shiny as blackest silk and skin as luminous as snow. She was cultured and highly intelligent. This was the courtesan Daji. What the Emperor did not know would be that this beautiful paragon of femininity would be the catalyst that would cause the downfall and destruction of the Shang Dynasty

Originally Daji or Su Daji was born a noblewoman of the House of Yousu, and she had indeed been a rare and beautiful educated girl.

Other, supernatural eyes had their eyes on her, waiting for its opportunity to prey on the young beauty and possess her body. This creature was a Fox Spirit with a malicious and evil nature that delighted in chaos and suffering. One day she had her chance, driving out the soul of the innocent young girl, the evil fox had its vehicle for interacting with human society and unleashing misery. With her cunning, and knowing her irresistible plans, off she went to the court of the Emperor.

As soon as the Emperor saw her he was infatuated. As is known the fox can *ensorcell* her chosen victim with her glamour and sheer sexual charisma. Emperor Zhou began to focus solely on Daji, attending to every need and tiny whim. Every minute away from her was torture and to see her unhappy or her wishes unfulfilled was like a nail through his heart.

Soon, the affairs of the Kingdom of Shang were left unexamined and neglected. The once noble character of the King began to coarsen.

Being a Fox, Daji demanded to be surrounded by animals. Soon the Emperor, rather than feeding the people and ensuring their security, built a zoo in fabled Xanadu, filled with the rarest birds and creatures known to mankind at that time.

One day while at the Temple of the creator mother Nuwa, rather than reverence, he lusted for the goddess's slim figure and milk laden breasts and questioned how it would be to drive deeply into the loins of the goddess. The goddess, angered, decided it was the Emperor's fate to be the last of his line.

Court life became an orgy of violence and sexual depravity, often against the will of the courtesans. Daji was now promoted to his favourite concubine and in lilting female laughter, revelled in the chaos.

In one famous orgy, the Emperor ordered a lake to be constructed and filled with wine, and an island in the middle was planted with trees from whose branches hung hunks of delicious cured meats. Participants were naked, chasing each other through this coppice of meats, reaching down into the lake to quench their thirst from the wine that lapped the shores, before carrying on with their fornications.

Encouraged by Daji, musicians were hired to create new pornographic songs set to music that seemed to reflect the wild thrusting of passion and the explosion of orgasm.

Daji loved to hear the screams of those tortured by cruelty. One typical torture was a brazen barrel filled with burning hot coals and set above a pit of fire. As the Emperor and Daji sat watching on their thrones, innocent men were forced to walk on the slippery curved surface of the barrel. One slip meant death by a painful fiery roasting on the searing flames below. As the victim stood on the barrel, the barrel would become hot. The victim would inevitably begin a kind of crazy dance on the barrel. Like a cruel schoolgirl, hand cupped over her cherry lips mouth she would laugh at their predicament, and soon the Emperor would join in.

Daji displayed a cruel, intelligent curiosity. She once had a pregnant woman cut open so she could see how it worked inside. She caused the death of a Minister famed for his wisdom and goodness just so she could see what a good man's heart looked like.

However, as the Shang kingdom sank into Caligula like depravity, it also became weak and vulnerable and its disgruntled people.

On the borders, Jiang Ziya, fully aware of Daji's nature, had mustered an army. The Battle of Muye led to the old Emperor throwing himself onto a fire. As for Daji, it is said that the wise Jiang used a peachwood sword to drive the cunning and cruel fox spirit from her body. No one can be sure.

However, according to the Far Eastern occult tradition that same fox spirit that had possessed the unfortunate maiden Daji fled to India.

No one can know quite what evils she had committed in India. What we do know is that she entered the Magadha Kingdom and had become a consort of one of the princes. A prolific author on tantra and other topics, Mogg Morgan, suggests this Indian incarnation of the Nine-Tailed Fox may well be Tishyarakshita. She was the final wife of Emperor Ashoka who was to Buddhism as Constantine was to Christianity. Among other things, she was famed for her cruel and inhuman medical experiments on some of her subjects. In another incident, bored with the aged Emperor she turned her attention to his son Kalapa. Kalapa was famed for the beauty of his eyes. However, when the prince spurned her attentions, she had his eyes removed and sent to her for her to enjoy without their now blinded and disfigured owner. Ultimately she caused the death of over a thousand innocent men. After her wicked machinations in India, she returned to China, possessing the maiden Bao Si.

Now Bao Si we do know something about. She existed in the Zhou Dynasty and became the favourite consort of King You.

She was said to have been the most beautiful maiden anyone can imagine, and to this day her beauty is proverbial.

In China, there is the concept of the Four Beauties, four historical women famed for their utter ravishing loveliness. In a traditional Chinese quatrain, it is said that the four beauties can cause 'fish to sink, birds to drop from the sky, the Moon to hide and the flowers to be shamed'. Though not one of the Four Beauties many would consider her an official fifth.

When presented at court the familiar pattern presented itself. The King, named You, was instantly enamoured and fascinated, so much so, he abandoned his then wife, Queen Shen. This would lead to the end of the Zhou Dynasty in the 7th century BCE.

Bao Si, though beautiful, was a deep and melancholy girl who rarely laughed. Concerned by her sadness, the King offered a considerable quantity of ingots of gold to anyone who could raise a smile or laugh on that gorgeous but tragic face.

In true fairy tale tradition, nothing could make the princess smile. Then one day, one of the court advisors suggested that they could light the beacons on the nearby hills that were normally used in emergencies to call neighbouring ally armies.

The beacons were lit and Bao Si cried with girlish delight as armies of men from those various kingdoms came thundering in on their sturdy warhorses.

Meanwhile, Bao Si had a son, Bo Fu, and the Emperor unwisely cut off the children of his former marriage to Queen Shen. A war broke out with the well-armed troops of Queen Shen's father invading the Kingdom of Zhou.

The king ordered the beacons to be lit to call support. No one came, since they did not take the call seriously as they had so many times been lit for the amusement of pretty little Bao Si.

The King was defeated, and legend says that the fox spirit, knowing the dainty mortal body had served its purpose, hung herself. That cunning vixen with the nine tails fled to Japan.

The wily spirit entered the body of a baby girl that had been left abandoned by the road. She was found and adopted by two loving parents who named her Mikizume. She was highly intelligent and by seven years old could recite difficult tracts of Japanese song and poetry. The fox spirit (kitsune in Japanese) was again hatching her plans even as she masqueraded in the body of the young girl.

Famed for her ability in poetry she was introduced to the court of Emperor Toba (1105-1156 CE). The Emperor and all the court were captivated and delighted by her performance, so much so she was made a permanent member of the court.

Mikizume grew to be a beautiful maiden and was renamed Tamamo No Mae. literally Lady Duckweed.

The first inklings of her supernatural nature occurred on her eighteenth birthday. She was required to give a poetry and song recital to the gathered court.

During her recital there was a sudden storm, a wind moaned through the court extinguishing all the candles and lamps in the palace. However, the beautiful Tamamo seemed to glow with a breathtakingly lovely iridescence that filled the court with light. It was deemed that the fair maiden was spiritually blessed by the heavens. Little did they know that in fact, it was the wily, thousands of years old nine tail fox, enchanting them to their coming destruction.

The old Emperor took a fancy to the beautiful Tamamo. There had never been such an ethereal beauty in his court as her. Her black hair piled up in the fashion of the time revealed a long neck that accentuated her grace. Her pale snow-like skin was without a single blemish. The eyes were large and almond-shaped and the mouth small yet sensuous. The Emperor spent all her days and nights with the maiden. Yet others noticed that he was falling under her control, this wasn't merely love but an obsession.

Tamamo No Mae

これを投よとよ

正月十一日

乙亥

應永二年

源翁和尚

獣となりて

觸れよて

この化たるよて

北上あり老孤

下野國那須

殺生石は

殺生石

In lovemaking, the maiden fulfilled his every desire and desires beyond which he had ever known. Yet instead of invigorating, the sex was destroying him. The kitsune was draining him of his essence. Tamamo seemed to become even more beautiful, but with every entry into her 'jade cave', he weakened. Soon the Emperor became so ill that it was obvious to all the court. Finally, he could not even raise himself from the royal cot.

However, attached to every court were occult specialists. These were the followers of The Way of Yin and Yang, the Onmyoji. Skilled in the arts of divination and spells. One of these Onmyoji was named Abe No Yasuchiba. He examined all the signs and at once knew Lady Tamamo for what she was. Yet he also knew that he should be cautious.

He praised Tamamo for her spiritual attainment and beauty and invited her to a special Onmyodo ceremony called the Taizan Fukun No Sai. This ancient ceremony was developed in Taoist China. It is the most powerful and revered of all Onmyodo ceremonies and was said to be able to even revive the dead. The central idea is to call Lord Taizan, and the gods of death to

The Killing Stone

lengthen the life of a sick individual.

The Onmyoji and the fox maiden sat to perform the ritual and proceeded to chant the ritual and offer the letter of request to the gods. Near the climax, the young maiden suddenly gasped and in the blink of an eye vanished before all the spectators. Her nature had been revealed to the astonishment of the assembled courtesans.

After this incident, two Samurai Lords were dispatched to catch Tamamo. The Samurai eventually traced Tamamo to Tochigi Province in Japan, alerted by rumours of missing women and children. He cleanly chopped off the physical body of the ancient Kitsune. Immediately her spirit leapt into a rock still now known as Sessho Seki, the Killing Stone where it can still be visited today.

.

Dakini As The Origin Of The Fox

I believe that the origin of the Fox spirit as we know her today originated from two streams of thought, the aboriginal and shamanic practices of the Chinese and the idea of the initiating, wisdom spirit known in Sanskrit as the Dakini. Before venturing back to China I must ask the reader to join me over the Himalayas in far-away India where the Dakini cult first originated.

Dakinis are primarily deities of Tantra. They are envisioned as wild witches with the capability to transform the tantric yogi who interacts with them. They are by no means peaceful and passive feminine spirits but wild, often naked with hair loose and full of libido. They are dangerous and yet offer the greatest possibility of transformation. Like all true initiations, they are beings of the in-between and straddle the gnosis of sex and death. The Dakinis are overtly sexual and erotic in the most active way possible. Their initiations are often given sexually.

Though well known in India it was the Tantric forms of Buddhism that seemed to have preserved the practice in Vajrayana or tantric forms of Buddhism

The Dakinis are intimately associated with the practice of tantric yoga in Tibet and Nepal. As embodiments of raw feminine power.

In tantric yoga, the Dakini is a kind of initiatrix. Initially, she may test the dedication and resolve of the yogi. Her image is passionate and sexual. Most images of a Dakini show her as a nubile young woman with her hair dishevelled as if in the throes of passion, nearly naked aside from jewelled hip girdles, bangles, armlets and necklaces and often holding a skull bowl, kapala, filled with menstrual blood.

The yogin, if successful, receive certain siddhis or magical powers from his Dakini. In practice as well as invocations to her, he will visualise the Dakini to the point she becomes seemingly real. He can touch her, see her and smell her and even feel the weight of the Dakini's caresses.

She is strongly associated with energy work in terms of the awakening of the mystical fire said to be latent in every human being. Once awoken, this mysterious energy rises through various Nadis or etheric 'arteries' and reaches certain centres (khorlo or chakras) to not only bring about illumination and ecstatic bliss but also give rise to siddhis (occult powers).

This whole process probably hearkens back to very ancient practices among the shamans. The sacred relationship of the spirit lover. For example, among the ancient Chinese, the Wu Shaman, whether male or female, dressed in beautiful clothes and wooed the spirits and gods. The relationship between shaman and spirit was that of a lover and the beloved. These ancient Wu shaman incantations sound like love poems filled with passionate yearning. If successful in their wooing, dressed in their finery and uttering beautiful songs, poetry, dance and music, a trance of pure ecstasy was reached and they would find himself or herself before the beloved who would transport them to a mysterious spiritual dimension. Once there the shaman would learn certain magical secrets or cures to help the tribe.

The magical fire raised in the yoga of the Dakini is also an ancient signature of old shamanic practices. Magical power has long been associated with the sensation of heat, a factor we shall later return to.

In essence, the magical power inherent in man is raw and unrefined sexual energy. This sexual energy in Chinese thought is known as Jing or Essence. By certain mental processes, this raw Jing can be refined into pure magical energy, at first to an intermediate energetic state known as Qi (steam, breath, gas) and finally as pure spiritual energy called Shen.

Tibetan yoga has a similar outlook. The raw sexual energy is often symbolised as a 'Burning' or 'Hot Girl' who is caused to 'awaken' and ascend the central channel or Sushumna. As she ascends she becomes increasingly refined and powerful, awakening the psychic abilities and transcendent capabilities of the yogin.

In the Chinese Neigong (yogic alchemy) traditions sexual arousal is a common way to produce or stimulate the raw sexual jing needed as the basic 'mercury' for transmutation. Neigong texts, mostly written for men, advise masturbation without ejaculation, before refining.

The Dakini is a muse invoked to create such sexual stimulation. Indeed in actual practice, a real partner is used in both Tibetan rites and Chinese 'Double Cultivation' alchemy. A male lacks the feminine power and therefore she is invoked to complete the circuit so to speak.

I believe this Dakini gnosis is a key component in the rituals and mythos of the Nine-Tailed Fox as we shall see.

If the Dakini is associated with the erotic component, she is also associated with another component, that of death. In other words, the Dakini is a gateway to both the mysteries of Eros, the Red Mysteries and the Mysteries of Thanatos, the White Mysteries. I say white and not black, because in Chinese symbolism, white is the colour of death, and lo, the Nine-Tailed Fox is always pale skinned and wearing long flowing white robes reminiscent of Chinese funerary robes.

How did the Dakini become associated with the fox? That is easily answered. In ancient India, tantrics would call these transformative female spirits in cremation grounds, shmashana. One of the symbolic animals of the crematorium was the jackal. The jackal became a kind of symbol of the yoginis, Dakinis and even Tara Shmashana herself. Jackals not being native to China became the fox.

The Fox In China

In China, the spirit fox is known as Hu Li Jing. We cannot be quite sure when her devotions began, but evidence seems to point to North-East China as the starting point of her cultus. Scholars almost certainly believe it came from primal shamanic beliefs where animal spirits were a focus.

The first mention of the Nine-Tailed Fox (Jiu Wei Hu) appears to have been 'The Classic of Seas and Mountains' (Shan Hai Jing). This is a work presenting a kind of Chinese bestiary of fabulous creatures living throughout a fantastical country loosely associated with real Chinese geography written around 400 BCE.

We read that the Nine-Tailed Fox is a companion of the mighty and beautiful Queen Mother of the West. This in itself is a very interesting statement. The Queen Mother of the West is one of the oldest continuously revered goddesses in the known world, with her description found on oracle bones dating back to 1500 BC. Originally due to her shamanic origins, the Western Mother, Xiwangmu, had a more animalistic appearance with tiger's teeth and leopard attributes. Later images show her as a beautiful Queen in the Tang Dynasty style. She lives in a paradise on Mount Kunlun, the Axis Mundi mountain of Chinese belief where she has the fabulous garden that includes the Peaches of Immortality. It is in her role as the Goddess of Immortality that the Nine-Tailed Fox accompanies the noble goddess of Kunlun.

This is important in relation to Lady Fox's role in certain alchemical and sexo-alchemical practices.

We learn that the Nine-Tailed Fox is a good omen, the nine tails representing abundance and plenty, especially in terms of fertility and progeny.

The Classic of Mountains and Seas tells us that the Nine-tailed Fox can be found in the Green Hills north of Tianwu and north of the Sunrise Valley. In this land, so-called because of the abundance of jade there, the Fox emits a sound like the cry of a baby, and eating of it protects one from the dreaded Gu poison.

Gu poison was a much-dreaded kind of black magic popular in China (and still exists to this day). Gu typically created from certain insects such as the giant centipede, serpents, spiders, lizards and toads was used as a method to control people. Notoriously it was used in Mihun, a kind of witchcraft used to mesmerise a potential lover into a "Stepford Wife" (more commonly used by women on men actually) submissive.

That the Nine Tail Fox has power over this kind of poisonous and controlling love magic is also interesting. As we shall see, the Nine Tail Fox is the very embodiment of glamour, sexual mastery and bewitchment.

A devotee of the Fox Lady is usually a master of love magic, sexual alchemy, fascination and transformation as well as having mastery and insight into the 'twilight world', the Yin World or Yin Mountain of ghosts.

The mighty Nine-Tailed Fox, unlike many supernatural beings, is said to begin as a humble fox. It is a common misconception that the fox begins as a human being. The fox, as we have seen, is considered a very yin animal in Asian thought. The fox lives in the outskirts of the village or town, occasionally encroaching on human territory. The fox is a creature of the twilight and the night and its cry is hauntingly melancholic. It is therefore a magical animal imbued with Yin virtues. The fox was often seen or built its nests in graveyards imbuing it with even more mystique. The cemetery is frequently associated with acts of magic used to call upon the powers of the Yin World. That the fox frequented the graveyards and even lived in tombs gave the impression that the fox was in a sense cultivating even more yin virtue than it already naturally possessed.

Interestingly, the fox living in a cemetery is not mere

superstition. Foxes are still frequent in graveyards here in the United Kingdom, even living in tombs. Several local councils around the United Kingdom exhibited concern when such fox homes caused graves to subside. Luckily in our more ecologically minded era, foxes are tolerated or even beloved in our country and urban settings, even in cemeteries.

It was then all these qualities that singled out the fox as that creature most prone to supernatural influence, perhaps compounded with lore that trickled in from India.

The scholar Guo Pu (276-234 CE) tells us that when a fox is fifty years old, having cultivated itself, it can transform into a woman. When it reaches the age of one hundred it can become a beautiful woman and a witch, some become men or can seduce men. They can know events that occur thousands of miles away and are masters of witchcraft, causing people to '... be beguiled and lose their senses'. When they are a thousand years old they can communicate with the Heavens and so become heavenly foxes.

The fox is thus believed to be cultivating a kind of immortality we usually associate with the practising Taoists. The fox grows from an animal state to that of absolute immortality. Though in this endeavour there is the risk of the wrath of heaven.

The age of the fox in question is usually the primary means of ascertaining its attributes and powers as seen in the above quote from Guo Pu.

In their evolution to becoming a Heavenly Fox, a Hu Xian (Fox Immortal or Fox Fairy) they inevitably reach the stage of appearing as, and interacting with, human beings. Sometimes in this stage, they have not quite mastered the ability to assume the form, and a person can spot some tell-tale sign of their incomplete transformation, usually to their utter shock. We can recall the tale of a wine-soaked scholar finding the beautiful maid in his bed, the lights dimmed and her lithe body stays hidden beneath the silken sheets. He reaches in and feels the soft skin and gentle feminine curves and suddenly he winces as he feels the bushy tail between his fingers. Or a passerby will walk with a beautiful woman holding her parasol and exquisite kimono that accentuates the fox's beauty only to look down and see, not the gentle shoed feet of a Japanese Cinderella but a pair of fox's feet padding on the ground!

The scholars of the Ancient Far East tell us more about how the fox cultivates her abilities and transformation to a celestial nature.

The cultivating fox is believed to draw upon the celestial energies of the Sun and Moon, drawing in those energies to form a core of immortality. Sometimes this core of immortal perfection is symbolised by a pearl that somehow encapsulates the power of the fox. This 'Fox Pearl' is said to be hidden and jealously guarded by the Fox Spirit. If a mortal should ever take it from her he could possess the means of immortality, magical power or even the control and destruction of the fox herself.

Both of these methods are immediately recognisable to the Taoist alchemist. Absorbing the Sun and Moon Essence are still basic training exercises in Taoist magic and can be found in the

Buddha Pearls

practical part of this book as part of the 'Fox Yoga'. The pearl is a representative of congealed magico-alchemical energy in Chinese literature somewhat like the Philosopher's Stone in Western Hermetic form.

The Fox Pearl is the very same pearl formed in Taoist adepts within the body by processes of internal yoga. In advanced practitioners, it becomes a real, solid object. Again this can be compared with the 'immortal bone' or luz of the Qabalists and the Buddha Pearl said to physically manifest in the bodies of those who reach Buddhahood. These relics are called *sarira* among Buddhist followers. When a monk is cremated the ashes are sifted, the mortician finding these telltale crystalline formations. The pearls are then kept in a reliquary designed for the purpose and are said to hold special powers to bless and heal.

This indestructible essence, the Pearl of Immortality is one of the goals of Taoist alchemy. In fact in the lore of the Immortal Fox, she is said to be a teacher of the alchemical arts and gives the gift of the pearl to her followers. We do not mean this as a metaphor, it is said she will literally visit the Taoist practitioner with a contract for him or her to sign and an actual pearl that must be swallowed by the alchemist.

As well as imbibing the essence of the Moon our apprentice fox spirit would perform a ritual with the human skull as its focus. The fox would place the skull on its head and perform meditations upon the seven stars of the Big Dipper, or some say the Pole Star. Cultivating in this way the fox would eventually be able to transform herself into a human being.

Of course, another method for the advancing fox to cultivate her energy was by sex with men. By certain sexual techniques, the cunning fox would tap into and drain the Yang essence of the man into her energetic system and store it for use in her occult progression.

This is a well-known technique in the Taoist sexual arts. Usually, the male would select a young woman to withdraw some of her Yin energy to make up for the fact that he, as a man, has less Yin energy than women. Women had similar practices in which they would draw on the Yang energies of virile men to enhance their own alchemy. In ancient times the practice was somewhat slyly done, the sorcerer stealing or rather vampirising the Yin essence of the feminine to reach greater androgyny of energy. The same was for the female adepts, who would often work as 'Flower Girls' or 'Sing Song Girls', polite euphemisms for sex workers, whose aim was to steal the Jing of their blissfully ignorant clientele.

However, among true adepts, such 'sexual vampirism' was a consciously shared act of Taoist yoga.

These sexual cultivation techniques are known as Double Cultivation in Taoism and form part of the gnosis of the devotees of the Nine-Tailed Fox.

The skull symbolism, and the Fox's mastery and even rivalry with the Realm of Ghosts point to her as being a gateway to the mastery of the Mysteries of Death.

In Taoist thought, we can essentially divide existence at its most basic level into the Yang World and the Yin World.

The Yang World is the world of existence, light and life. The Yin World is that of death and negative existence. The two worlds are by no means completely separate.

The Fox symbolises their point of intersection, the twilight of existence. Women are the gate of birth and to the great glamour and illusion of the Wheel of Life. Yet, at the very moment of life, the process of death begins. In Taoist thought the newly born infant is filled with Heavenly Yang energy brought fresh from the pre-birth state referred to as the Pre-Heaven State. The moment we are born we begin leaking our life slowly but surely. We are now in the Post-Heaven State. Yet Taoists teach that this process can be slowed and even, more rarely, halted so a kind of immortality is achieved, the state of the Immortal or Xian. Yet we should not necessarily think or confuse this with physical immortality.

Sex and death are therefore the two mysteries that are revealed by the Fox Immortal, for sex and death are two sides of the same coin. The experience of both is the greatest transformers of human consciousness in most genuine systems of magic. This is a key theme in the higher Mysteries of Fox Magic.

For the average villager not initiated into the Mysteries of the Fox, it was something simultaneously feared and loved. At one time nearly every home had an altar to the Fox Spirits and every Temple had a hidden or nearly hidden, often octagonal chamber for the worship of the Fox.

Officially, the academics and scholars frowned on the secret rites of the Fox. Some even had altars devoted to the ancient Fox that we know historically as Daji, the wanton, kingdom shattering Fox who came to be known as Tamamo in Japan. Daji's devotion became so widespread in China that a government edict was issued to outlaw the practice.

The Fox Cult had, as we mentioned, a large following in North-East China.

The Fox was the most prominent in a cultus known as the Bei Ma, which translates roughly as the Northern Horses. This cult has an origin lost in time, but judging by its practices and belief structure it seems to have originated from local shamanistic based practices.

The cult in fact has many spirits connected with animals and other spirit beings, but the Fox Family was and still is considered the most powerful of them all. The Beima cult included Yellow Weasel, Hedgehog, Bear, Wolf, Tiger and Python, Ghost and Bird spirits among its possible possessing spirits. Traditionally divination methods were done by the local peoples to ascertain what spirit family they should devote themselves to. Sometimes one was connected to a particular clan by ancestral linkage over many lifetimes. Adherents sometimes tell tales where a particular individual refused to acknowledge his spiritual clan only to become unfortunate or terribly ill and he or she acknowledged and devoted himself to the spirits. In the ceremonies, the Beima devotee is temporarily possessed by the spirit and exhibits all the signs of the creature. For example, the python possessed individual is writhing on the ground. While possessed messages will be given and powers obtained.

In Beima the Fox Family is fairly complex, with Fox Auntie and Uncle and various other family members. The Fox family is considered the most powerful of the Beima spirits due to their ancient lineage of Taoist wisdom and cultivation.

The Fox is thus one of the most ancient and primary spirits of the ancient Chinese. We can see that there are several kinds of foxes. Some are dreaded and some are beloved, but all generally misunderstood by western culture.

One Taoist priest noted that the fox gives us what we deserve. The fox tests her devotees. In invoking or experiencing the fox she (or indeed he in some cases) takes the form of an incredibly beautiful and seductive person. If the Taoist scholar succumbs in pure lust he is said to be consumed by her, literally bled dry of his jing essence until there is nothing left except a dying husk of his former self. However, should he resist her temptations he has everything to gain in terms of alchemical cultivation.

The fox can also possess the individual causing wild fox-like behaviours such as eating raw meat and craving the fried bean curd so beloved of the fox. We shall look closer at this aspect in the Japanese lore of the fox spirit, there called the Kitsune.

The fox is a dangerous spirit to work with but also the one with greater and faster rewards. Lore also tells us that beyond mere lust it is also possible for there to be love, marriage and even children in marriages between fox spirits and human beings. Again I point to our western lore of the fay folk and elementals in the Comte de Gabalis tradition for an almost exact parallel in this tradition.

In China, some people believe that people with the surname Hu, may in fact be descendants of such a fox-human 'fairy 'marriage' that occurred in the mountainous regions of Northern China.

Now we must turn our attention to the most famous of the Fox Immortal Temples in old China. To this day most real fox ceremonies of Chinese origin are orientated to or contain references to this Temple, in a sense we could say it is the Mecca or Jerusalem of the Fox Tradition. To the magically minded folk, it is the magical nexus or powerpoint from which the energies of the Supreme Fox Immortal radiate.

On the beautiful twin peaks of the Dragon Tiger Mountain or Longhu Shan, there is a temple called the Heavenly Master Temple. If the bold traveller climbs up to that Temple he will, if he searches, find there a fairly unprepossessing little side Temple known as the Fox Hall. This is one of the few truly ancient fox temples remaining in China today that is accepted by Taoist orthodoxy. Though there are many secret Fox cults, temples and shrines scattered throughout Asia, they are not part of official Taoism. In the author's opinion, this doesn't negate their power or lineage. Indeed some of these unorthodox lineages, thriving in relative secrecy and remaining unrecognised by Taoist orthodoxy, have often preserved the old ways better than official Taoism.

Now enter the Fox Hall and you will immediately be struck by the thick clouds of incense and sheer potent vibrancy of the place. There on the altar are statues of the Huxian. She is beautiful, with thick black hair and a yellow dress. Another image shows her riding upon a fox. That is the Fox Maiden, the Blessed Lady Huxian. There is a legend of how she reached this Temple.

It was during the Northern Song Dynasty and the powerful but gruff Ancestral Master was meditating in the temple grounds.

Suddenly, quite out of nowhere, huge menacing looking clouds began to form in the skies above, dangerously black with the blood-red tint that seemed to make those clouds even more threatening. The Master looked at them with suspicion. He knew the times and seasons, had meditated for many years to tune into the flow of the Dao and its heavenly and earthly cycles. Immediately he knew there was something wrong. He guessed that there was demonic activity afoot. Unperturbed he went back to his meditations. He knew that conditions for meditating were not always perfect and relished the challenge of focusing his mind despite the brewing storm.

Soon the intense atmospheric tension broke. Thunder clapped loudly across the lakes and mountains, bolts of lightning pierced the earth in tremendous violent flashes that shook the very ground upon which he sat.

The Master, though he had his eyes closed, suddenly felt the presence of another lifeform in the room. There was an energetic shift in the Qi field. Still, he did not acknowledge its presence and remained in his meditations. There was a whimpering and soft weeping. The Master opened his eyes and there standing before him, was perhaps the most beautiful woman he had ever seen. She was dressed in a gown of yellow silk that accentuated a figure that was designed to seduce. Her pale skin was white and her lips like cherry blossoms on snow. The thick silken hair was loose. Beauty like this could not be mortal.

"Who are you, or should I say what are you!" the gruff old Master demanded.

There was a long pause as the girl tried to gather herself amid her tears, and she began to tell her story.

"Master of Dao, please forgive me. I only seek your help and counsel. I am a Fox Spirit, who has cultivated for over 2000 years. As my power grew, the Heavens became aware of my potential and they grew afraid of my power and my potential. The High Lord, the Jade Emperor has set a bounty on my life and he has sent the Thunder Gods to kill me. This is the storm that you now see and hear in this place. I had nowhere to run or to hide. Forgive me, Master, I sought refuge here in this holy place and in your august presence, knowing that the Thunder Lords would never strike this place."

The Master looked at her sternly, "Begone Lady, you have raised the wrath of Heaven!"

The young beauty burst into tears once more, and then between stuttering sobs continued her heartfelt pleas, "O Master, I care not for my own life. Within my womb, a child grows. If I am killed my innocent child will be killed with me."

The Master felt compassion, this girl was not thinking of herself but the life of another, clearly this was not the Fox Spirit intent on destruction or vampirism.

"Good lady, do not fear, I shall myself intercede on your behalf with the Jade Emperor, but you must make a solemn vow here and now. Firstly you shall not eat foods derived from living creatures, secondly, you shall live far from human beings and isolate yourself from them, and thirdly you shall continue your Dao cultivation to the benefit and merit of all those who know you".

Dragon Tiger Mountain

The Fox Spirit agreed. The Master spoke to the Jade Emperor himself. And as if by magic the black clouds that darkened the land dissolved and the skies once again shone with an azure brilliance that only the air of mountains can reveal.

The Fox Spirit retreated to a hidden spot somewhere in the famously beautiful Yuntai Mountains. Her child was a daughter, Xiao Bai Xian, the Little White Immortal, who would also become famous for her beauty.

To this day many disciples of the Fox Lady will go to her Temple to offer her incense and flowers and wish for prosperity and fortune, especially in terms of increased beauty, love and improved popularity.

As we shall see later, it is very auspicious for the devotee of the Fox Lady to obtain some ash from the incense burner of her thurible in the Fox Hall on Longhu Mountain.

From ancient China, there emerged many Fox methods, the teaching and use of which shall be taught later in this book. On a superficial level, the devotee of the Fox will have certain enhanced abilities, especially in attracting people and in the sexual arts, but at a higher level, the Fox Cult has far more profound mysteries that take the devotee deeper into the Dao. These secrets shall also be explored and hinted at for those who have eyes to see and ears to listen.

The Fox Cult has, in particular, a large following among Asian entertainers, singers, actresses and actors as well as distraught lovers and sex workers. There are numerous speculations in the Chinese language press on which actress or actor is using what occult practice to further their career. However, strange as it seems, many Chinese find themselves going to Thailand to find Nine Tail Fox Talismans, completely forgetting that it is a Chinese tradition! In our next Chapter however we look towards Japan, for several of the Fox Cult Mysteries are revealed there.

Huxian image at Fox Hall.

Kitsune
The Fox Cult In Japan

We cannot be entirely sure when the Fox Cult arrived in the Land of the Rising Sun from China. Probably, Japan already had some native traditions concerning the fox. Shinto, the indigenous religion of Japan, is essentially animistic in nature. All things are imbued with life and have a soul and intelligence ... the wind, the stones, the mountains and so forth. The rich lore of Kami

Images of Lady Huxian

Images of Lady Huxian in Asian cinema and television.

Lady Huxian in Fox Hall

(spirits) in Shinto would surely have contributed or added to the lore of the Fox.

We may recall the tale of Tamamo No Mae which in itself implies a transmission of the Fox Cult to Japan from China.

This was likely during an enlightened period of cultural exchange between China and Japan that reached its peak in the Tang Dynasty. Many of the customs and iconic images we associate with Japan today are adapted from Tang Dynasty culture, which was held in high esteem across Asia at that time.

The kimono, the classic piled hair and white makeup with red-tinted eye corners and ruby small lips of the Japanese courtesan were adaptations of Tang lady fashions. The tea ceremony, martial arts, literature, and calligraphy were all brought to Japan from China.

However, it was not just high courtly fashion and literature that found its way into Japan but also the magical arts and mystical beliefs.

The most famous example would be the nine mudras of Kuji-In. These began as a kind of empowering defensive and attacking magic used by Taoist wizards who had to traverse dangerous paths through the mountains and feared the Yin beings, ghosts and demons who might take an interest in them. Probably it had passed to a similar wilderness loving mountain hermit movement in Japan called the Yamabushi. The Yamabushi generally follow a kind of esoteric Buddhism called Shingon. Without a doubt, such techniques of battle magic and invisibility would have been interested in a technique like the nine mudras. Most people would be aware of these 'magical hand signs' from Japanese ninja movies and anime from where they entered popular culture.

In analysing Japanese mysticism we need to bear in mind three streams of influence.

The first stream is the native Japanese one, beliefs and concepts developed among the native Japanese peoples themselves. Shinto is the natural home of these native beliefs, though even there we can see a Chinese influence.

The second stream is the Chinese influence. This is apparent in arts such as The Way of Yin and Yang or Onmyodo. Onmyodo was essentially a kind of Japanese Taoism and derived much of its technique and even its deities from aspects of Taoism such as the Yin and Yang classics, the Five Elements classics, Feng Shui and divinatory arts such as Qimen Dunjia, Astrology and especially Da Liu Ren.

The third stream is what we could loosely term the Indian by way of Buddhism. Though Zen Buddhism is the most well known among the sects, Japan has a rich tapestry of Buddhist Ryu (schools). In terms of esoteric and magical knowledge, the most important of these would be the so-called Tantric schools such as Shingon, Tendai and Mikkyo. Interestingly Japanese esoteric Buddhism itself blends Mahayana tantric Buddhism with some Taoist practices, such as the Kuji-In mentioned above.

Now, in terms of the Fox Cult we must note, that as in China, the fox spirits are considered both very wise and divine, or terrible spirits that can maliciously prey on humanity.

There are two mainstream and popular fox deities in Japan, and both are aspects or equivalents of the Chinese Huxian.

By far the most widespread is Inari or O-Inari, a Shinto goddess. In legends, the Japanese scribes record that at a time when humanity was still in its youth, there fell upon them a great famine. The people cried and starved, looking to the Heavens for aid with the dull relentless ache of hunger in their bellies. They're descended from the Heavens, a goddess in the form of a young and beautiful maiden riding upon a white fox and carrying a sheath of grain that was heavy with ripening seeds of rice. The people were saved.

As can be ascertained from this story of the arrival of Inari, she is a fox goddess, but also the goddess associated with fertility and agriculture. This is interesting because as we know from Huxian, she indeed represents and personifies the powerful forces of sexuality. In Japan Inari becomes the Goddess associated not only with rice but also tea, Sake and even blacksmithy.

The connection with the art of blacksmithing may seem like an odd one but as most occultists and folklorists will know, the blacksmith's art is a magical one. It is no accident that the earliest alchemists were associated with the art of the blacksmith, and the ancient neigong or inner alchemy itself is a descendent of blacksmith concepts. The fires of jing essence are mastered with the bellows of breath control.

Her temples are beloved in Japan and instantly recognisable for their vermilion Torii gates. You will often see a pair of white foxes with raised tails on either side of the gate. One is male and the other female. Sometimes one has a pearl of wisdom or medicine in its mouth and another has a scroll. These represent the inner secrets of the Tao. The scroll represents the method and the vows of the devotee in arts such as Daoist cultivation. The Pearl of the Fox or the Wish-Fulfilling Jewel is the product of that inner alchemy. In one legend successful invokers of the Fox Goddess will be visited by her messengers, the pure white kitsune, one male and one female. They will agree to and sign the scroll, which is said to be a vow. And then they are given the Pearl, a passed down portion of the cultivated Dao of the alchemical operations of the Fox spirits.

The second major Fox goddess in Japan comes from the Indian stream via esoteric Buddhism, she is named Dakiniten. Her very name confirms a link between the Fox Lady and the Dakini, a subject we discussed in a previous chapter. We also might note that images of Dakiniten riding a white fox accord with images of Huxian in the Fox Hall in the Hulong Temple in China.

In many ways, some of the more hidden mysteries of the Lady Fox Immortal are more clearly revealed. Dakiniten was said to have been brought into the fold of Japanese esotericism by the Tantric Buddhist researcher and reformer Kukai. She was quickly taken up by the Imperial family and a certain secret ritual was used in the coronation of Emperors, though it was later abandoned and fell into obscurity.

In Japanese lore, Dakiniten was said to eat the hearts of men from which she gained some mysterious power that bolstered her magic. Other scriptures imply that it was a kind of energy sometimes referred to as just 'the yellow'. Probably this refers to jing essence. Dakiniten means Heavenly Dakini. She is depicted as a beautiful girl holding a sword and/or a wish-fulfilling jewel and riding a white fox.

She was worshipped by her followers for great prosperity and fortune in life. However once one had dedicated one's self to her cult you had to conduct her rituals all your life. If you should stop you would lose everything and be plunged into disaster and ruin.

Her real mysteries, those that were so controversial in Japanese conservative society that they were banned and today only survive in mention and manuscript. I am here referring to the Tachikawa Ryu, a little known school of esoteric Buddhism that had Dakiniten as one of its chief deities. It had a combination of rites that employed not only sex but the death element, the skull, that was utilised in a necromantic manner.

Of course, the use of erotic and necromantic elements is pure Fox Spirit magic. You may recall that in the arts of transformation from a fox into a human, the fox employed a human skull and worshipped the Big Dipper. This controversial aspect of the Fox Mysteries is something we shall cover in practical detail later.

Kitsune Lore

There are many unique and charming aspects to the lore of the kitsune that seem to be unique to the island of the rising sun.

Kitsune, as in China, can be both charming and dangerous. They can be enemies that trick and deceive, they can be seductive lovers and powerful sorceresses, healers or killers.

The most famous magician of Japan, Abe No Seimei, the

Japanese Merlin if you will, was a master of the art of Onmyodo, the Way of Yin and Yang. Some scholars claim that his teacher was a nine-tailed fox, and some go as far as to say that the Nine-Tailed Fox was his mother.

The Kitsune of Japanese lore are both revered, loved and dreaded. There are stories of Kitsune repaying a kindness but equally bringing destruction. The highly cultivated foxes are termed Zenko, and usually, but not always show kindness towards the human race. They are usually very ancient intelligences who have self-cultivated spiritually. With each passing level of self-cultivation, a new tail grows. Finally, the status of Celestial Fox is achieved with the growth of a ninth tail and the fox fur transforms into white or gold.

The Yako on the other hand is the common fox spirit and is considered wild and uncultivated in comparison to the Zenko. Their nature tends to be more malicious in intent.

There was a time, especially during the Edo Period of Japanese history that the fox was a much-dreaded part of life. For men, this danger lay in this typical scenario. As he walked at night he might chance upon a seemingly beautiful woman. He may be charmed by her looks, her exquisite smile and her seemingly cultured conversation, her seductive lilting laughter as they pass down the dark narrow streets of Kyoto. They pass by a local friend's house and he comforts her as the neighbour's dogs yap wildly at the couple. Of course, the gentleman is unaware of the fact that the Kitsune has an antipathetic relationship with dogs. Dogs, with their sixth sense, are quick to respond to the aura of the kitsune.

The gentleman by now half-crazed with love in the enchanting company of his graceful companion, finds himself inviting her to his home to partake of warmed saki to remove the chill of the Japanese winter. Sitting together, singing old folk songs and discussing all manner of educated lore, they drink more and more rice wine to accompany their seemingly deepening passion. Suddenly, now a little drunk, the pale lady notices the young man's face agape in terror. In her inebriation, she had not held onto her human form as firmly as she should have. There swishing behind her wickedly is her fox tail!!!

To this day the word Kitsune can be applied to a particularly beautiful and charming woman, To be Kitsune-Gao or Kitsune Faced is to have a particular kind of beauty. This is the narrow face pointed like a melon seed and eyes tilted upwards at the corners, thin but well-shaped eyebrows and high cheekbones.

The Kitsune were also believed to have supernatural powers, no doubt arising from their long years in spiritual exercise and ability to penetrate the veils between this world and the world of the unseen. They could become invisible, transform into any form they choose though they favoured the form of a beautiful woman, could manifest in dreams, control the weather and create illusions of such realism that those who beheld them could not distinguish them from reality and even bending time and space itself.

Like the Chinese Hu Li Jing, the fox could also have the vampiric quality feeding on the life essence of the clueless man

she chose to feed upon to fortify her powers.

Kitsune could also possess people, usually women. This sickness was known as kitsunetsuki, an illness that was also well known in China. Ancient lore said that the essence of the fox would enter the young woman's body by her breasts or under the fingernails. Within a few days to a few weeks, the very facial expression of the young woman would warp to reveal a more fox-like face. The characteristic eyes slanting at the corners, the narrowing of the face, a more snout-like appearance to the mouth. She would have cravings for raw meat and the fried tofu packets filled with rice so beloved of foxes. They might speak and write languages that the simple girl had never learned, she might run naked through the streets yelping like a fox or exhibit uncharacteristic sexual promiscuity.

Usually, fox possession was a curse forced upon the unsuspecting girl but there are cases where this was done consciously. Indeed in some families, it was a tradition, recalling the Bei Ma Fox Cult of Northern China. Such Fox mediums were often fortune-tellers and healers.

A curious phenomenon of fox lore is foxfire. Fox fires or kitsunebi are balls of light, only a few centimetres across and usually red or orange, though blue has also been reported, that seem to dance around, usually in the countryside, forests and woods. Similar to the English lore of the will-o'-the-wisp or corpse lights they could lure travellers from the safety of the common path into danger. Sometimes whole strings of these lights were seen as if a procession of Kitsune were carrying brightly lit red lanterns. Traditional lore says however that the light is a manifestation of supernatural light emanating from the tail of the fox.

Another charming legend has it that whenever it rains on a sunny day and there is nary a cloud in sight, a kitsune is getting married.

Kitsune Dust is a magical powder that is used by kitsune to blow into the faces of those they wish to cast spells upon.

A Ritual To See The Kitsunebi, The Foxfire

So far we have given a potted history of the Kitsune/Hu Li Jing and not offered much in the way of practical work. Now magicians are or should be a practical bunch who like to roll up their sleeves. What follows are a few rituals from the Japanese Kitsune tradition. The first ritual allows you to access the liminal world of the Kitsune by evoking the vision of those little orbs of foxfire as described. Thank You to Kozou of the Shingon lineage for allowing me to share this ritual.

These simple little rituals are ideal to ease you into the world of Hu Li Jing. The magic and mystery of the Hu Li Jing is no light undertaking, if you break your vows to the Huxian/Dakiniten there is a great danger. This isn't something that a neopagan or chaos magician can just adopt off the cuff or haphazardly. This is a real and living tradition with its guardians and it must be respected. The foxfire ritual is therefore a good starting point to ease you into the shallow end of the deep pool of the Asian Fox Tradition.

The magician will need an altar, preferably something portable, two small vases, two small tea candles, an Asian style teacup, two small Chinese style bowls. One bowl contains salt and another bowl contains rice. A third bowl containing dried rice will be used for inserting three incense sticks. A small ceramic teapot. You will also need some mugwort and some flowers, such as foxgloves or bluebells.

The ritual generally takes place outside, perhaps in a meadow or at the edge of a wood or forest. Choose the day of a New Moon at the Zishi hour, ie 1-3 am.

The altar is laid down. The two vases are put at the back on the left and right. Put your flowers in them. The two candles are placed at each front corner. In the centre place a bowl of freshly cooked rice, a teacup to the right of the rice and the salt bowl to the immediate left. In front of this will be the incense bowl.

Light the two candles.

Step back from the altar with four steps, clap hands twice in front of your chest and bow. Then clap once more.

Return to the altar and light the three incense sticks, hold them between your two palms in a prayer-like gesture. Insert them into the dried rice of the incense bowl.

Put the mugwort in the teapot and add hot water and let it steep. I would recommend having hot water in a good thermos flask. Pour some of the freshly brewed mugwort tea into the cup. Take three steps back and bring palms to your chest. Say:

Asa kara yoru made watashitachi o mite.Anata no seishin wa kaze ni kakurete imasu, Yoru wa asobi ni kimasu, ningen no me kara hanarete odorimasu, WATASHI NO ME O ARITE, ANATA NO HONO O MISOTE KUDASAI !!

You may prefer to say this in English:

From morning and into the night you watch us. Your spirit hides in the wind. At night you come out to play. Away from the eyes of man, you can dance. OPEN MY EYES, SHOW ME YOUR FLAMES !!

The sentence said in capitals should be said three times.

Sit, take up the 108 bead rosary and say the following mantra 108 times:

KITSUNE TACHI GA KURUYO
(Come Kitsune)

Repeat the whole process four times. On the final time, sit and await the foxfire.

Blue orbs are young Kitsune.
Red orbs are kitsune who are 101 to 400 years old.

White orbs are kitsune who are 401 to 999 years old.

Golden orbs are kitsune that are over a thousand years old.

Since their trust must be earned you may not succeed the first time so don't feel disappointed. Try again another night.

Clap your hands and say thanks. Leave the food behind.

A Kitsune Spell Of Love Or Bewitchment

This is also, naturally, a spell from Japan and is popular with girls and boys who want to cast a simple love spell to obtain the favours of one whom they are attracted to. It is an example of mudra and breath magic. The use of the breath is frequent in Asian magical practice as it conveys or transmits Qi energy [Ki in Japanese]. The fox sorcerer or sorceress will, with their right hand, make the Kitsune mudra. The kitsune mudra literally looks like a fox's head. In appearance, it is similar to the 'rabbit' hand shape children use to make a shadow rabbit on a wall. Focusing on the hand, the practitioner imagines the red light of the kitsune gathering in the hand. When you feel it has accumulated enough energy, turn the handover and blow towards the beloved. Visualise this energy as if it is a sparkling stream of tiny particles reaching the heart of the target. This is the famous 'fairy fox dust'.

The Spell Of The Golden Sunrise Fox

Again thank you to Kozou, a priest of the Shingon and Mikkyo tradition for sharing and initiating me into this wonderful spell in the Japanese kitsune tradition.

This lovely fox ritual is used to communicate with a person telepathically. For example, you would appear in their dreams or when you are highly skilled, which can manifest as a kind of ghost or apparition before their eyes.

The sorcerer must first prepare by bathing and washing in hot water in which leaves of Yomogi have been steeped. Yomogi is simply mugwort, an important plant in most Chinese and Japanese systems for purifying and cleansing. Not only the body but the mouth is also rinsed with the mugwort steeped water.

Using a white towel or cotton cloth the magician now dries his body and dons a white robe, the so-called Robe of Death.

At the altar, the priest lights two white candles and three sticks of incense and sits before the altar.

On the altar should be an image of the Golden Nine-Tailed Fox or a tablet with her name written in Chinese characters and made of wood.

Taking some time to calm the mind with slow breathing and focusing on the centre of the altar. He or she forms a sword mudra with the right hand and places the tips of the fingers on the bottom lip. The left-hand forms a bowl-shaped palm to symbolise an offering bowl which is placed beneath the navel, which is the position of the psychic centre we call the Dantian in Daoism but Hara in Japanese.

The magician then whispers over the tips of the sword mudra "TENKO KURU". Note that Tenko is the Japanese word for the highest form of evolution for a Kitsune, the golden celestial form of a fox with nine tails. Its golden colour thus signifies the golden radiance of the rising sun.

The master continues reciting the mantra over and over again until he begins to have a sensation in the 'third eye' area between the eyebrows. This accumulates and builds up until there is a pressure that seemingly wants to burst.

At this point he or she envisions as realistically as possible and without himself, the golden fox entering the third eye area.

Once the fox spirit has been felt to truly enter the third eye, the occultist takes three deep breaths and relaxes the sword mudra from the lips but still maintaining the shape. The left hand now

also forms a sword mudra. Hold both swords to the lips and swipe them to the sides, left to the left side and the right hand to the right side and say: "SHUU".

The magician will have ready the following items. A traditional paper effigy in the Japanese style and a paper effigy of a fox. These should consist of thin white paper. Black ink infused with mugwort. Ideally, you need the name and date of birth of the person with whom you wish to telepathically communicate, and even better some Qi links such as nail clippings, a patch of cloth from their unwashed clothes, hair and so on.

With the paper doll and with the brush draw a pentagram (see illustration). Like in western magic, the pentagram represents the invocation of the five elements. Flip the effigy over and write the name and birthdate of the person with whom you wish to communicate. Also, draw a pentagram on the paper doll of the fox.

In Japanese, the magician writes 'kokoro hira te' meaning 'Your mind is open', and on the fox doll you write 'kokoro ni kokoro' (mind to mind). Note that these can also be translated as 'Your heart is open' and 'heart to heart'.

You will now close the effigy, having a photo, cloth or hair etc., of the target and placing or fixing the fox effigy over where the heart would be inside it. Sprinkle some mugwort on the paper doll which is on the altar. Burn three more sticks of incense.

Again, the occultist forms a sword mudra with his right hand and then draws a pentagram in the air above the effigy. Then return the mudra to your bottom lip and the left hand, again in the offering bowl gesture at your *dantian*. Focus on the point between your eyebrows, chanting:

(NAME OF TARGET): Wa rokoro o hiraki, kiite,
(NAME OF TARGET): (Open your heart/mind)

Repeat it again and again, visualising the Golden Fox with

nine tails leaving your third eye and entering the third eye of the target. You can then communicate with that person.

When you have finished, bring your left hand up into the sword mudra at the lips to join the right fingers. Swipe them apart as if opening a curtain and utter 'Shuu'.

Visualise the fox leaving you by the third eye and into the Fox Tablet, Statue or Image.

Finally take your time to thank the Fox and offer rice, tea and tofu.

The Hu Li Jing
In Modern Asia

One could be forgiven for thinking that somehow the fox cult is an ancient practice and that hu li jing are not part of modern culture. Look deeper and that is far from true. If you wander the slick urban streets of Hong Kong, or the space-age modernity of Singapore you will, if you are persistent, find her. It may be in a backstreet Fox temple. Entering therein you immediately see thick clouds of rich agarwood incense with its sweet but slightly musky odour. Agarwood is the traditional incense of the Fox Lady, not only for its Yin properties but because it is opulent and sensuous. You will see the predominant colour is red. There is an altar, draped in vermillion cloth and a strange red board inscribed with Chinese power words. You see women and men, hands in prayer gestures, bowing before statues and pictures of a beautiful woman dressed in white ... a fox at her feet. You have just found the Temple of the Fox.

The fox is an enduring if often shadowy part of Chinese culture but sometimes it still hits the news in China and within Chinese communities. Older generations report that denizens of the fox folk helped in the fight against Japanese soldiers in World War Two. A more modern and infamous example is the Fox panic of Hong Kong in the 1980s.

In 1981, in the Windsor Mall in the Causeway Bay area in Hong Kong, a shopkeeper desperate for more business decided to call seven fox spirits from a nearby banyan tree, known to be a fox spirit nest.

The very next day, according to urban legend, an image of a fox appeared overnight in the marble facade of the building.

Strange events started occurring, people were struck down with crippling illnesses and a baby was found dead in mysterious circumstances.

One couple staying on a romantic retreat in the Windsor Hotel drank wine under the moonlight.

Later that night, between sleep and waking, a woman woke up and saw another woman, beautiful but with red eyes shouting at her: "Why didn't you fucking toast me bitch!!!"

Another woman woke up, turned in her bed and saw the face of a fox leering at her, teeth bared. It became so bad the Windsor Hotel had to be exorcised and a feng shui expert called.

On a lighter note, and I've seen this myself, the eyes of those who worship and do the fox skin meditation have subtle changes to their shape, becoming more elongated and angled ... "Curiouser and curiouser" as Alice would say. The phenomenon was caught on TV over many weeks in Taiwan.

It is certainly true in the experience of many Huxian followers, that the eyes change to a more oblique and seductive appearance.

The Fox Immortal, Patron Of Movie Stars

The worship of the Fox Immortal is, so it is rumoured, popular among those in the Asian film and music industry, but only a few have publicly come out of the occult closet. One of these is Jessica Hsuan, born in Hong Kong and educated in Imperial College London, she became one of the famous 'Fa Dans' or young maidens of 1990s movies.

Xuan Xuan as she is known in the Chinese speaking community, became an open advocate of the Fox Immortal cult and appeared on Taiwanese television to show the changes it had created for her. She exclaims in her interview "I am now slimmer and my face is sharper, all the rotten peach blossoms are gone and the good peach blossoms are following ..." Peach blossom in Chinese means amorous men and women. In particular, she notes the effect on her career and her eyes.

那外来意识会｝曼｝曼
影响到该物质的重组

banyan tree was, according to a local Taoist priest, the origin of the fox spirit

e Windsor Mall

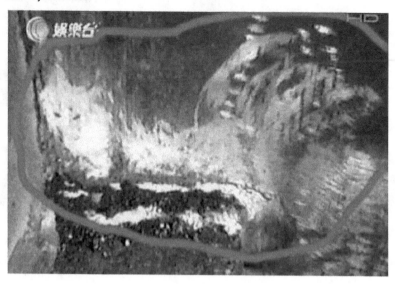

The fox image that appeared on the marble wall in the Windsor Mall.

Another popular tale of Fox magic that seemed to have a rather tragic ending is that of the singer Jinny Ng or Wu Ruo Xi. Apparently, she was a struggling young singer until her friend and confidante introduced her to the mysteries of fox magic. As you may recall, the Fox Immortal is popular in the entertainment industry as her devotees obtain the power to 'bewitch' their audiences with a certain glamour. I can attest to this power when it is truly mastered.

The problem was that she chose to engage in the practice in Thailand. To explain this further, the Nine Tail Fox Immortal is not or has ever been a spirit natural to Thai magic. This isn't a problem in itself but Thai magic is often based on necromancy, recruiting the spirits of the dead by spells and body parts of the dead called *prai*. Again this is not a problem by itself, but when the two combine you have spirits masquerading as something they are not. In other words, rather than the real Nine-Tailed Fox Immortal helping her career, she was using the souls of the dead.

Initially, it worked. She was suddenly thrown into the limelight and had a hit single. She was rich and beautiful, a male fantasy. Then things went wrong. There were small accidents, her father suddenly died of a stroke and so on. Soon her career floundered and she is now but a memory, more well known for her brush with the false fox cult and her tragic downfall than anything else.

After some weeks, Jessica reports a change in her appearance. According to her account, her face became more pointed and triangular and the eyes more beautiful and coquettish.

在自己的家裡拜大仙要脫衣服

Taiwanese movie star Jessica Hsuan presented a program on Huxian worship.

The singer Jinny Ng is now a famous story among those who enjoy a good supernatural yarn in Asia.

Ma Weiqing

Ma Weiqing

Ma Weiqing is a famous figure in Taiwan and Hong Kong. Why? Because she is one of the avatars of the Fox Immortal herself. She genuinely exhibits certain occult powers and is thus highly sought after by the rich and famous including movie stars and top business executives.

Her mother claims that one night, she had a strange dream. She dreamt there was a fox, covered in blood and suddenly it forced itself through her vagina into her womb after having bitten her right arm. She woke up from the terrible nightmare, and immediately went into labour, giving birth to Ma Weiqing. The day was the seventh day of the seventh month of the Chinese lunar calendar...the day when the Gate of Ghosts is opened.

Initially, Ma was a charismatic and popular student who easily passed her examinations by sometimes receiving answers or clues to her tests in dreams. She then became apprenticed to a local doctor of traditional folk medicine. Her powers of healing and sorting out love problems became legendary and still are.

Fox Magic
In The Luban Grimoire

The Luban is a curious volume that the elder generation of Chinese speaks about in hushed and dreaded whispers to their descendants. No one is quite sure about its origin though there are tales.

The Luban is a sorcerer's manual associated with what we could call a Chinese builder's guild but has long filtered out into Chinese magical society in the same way as say *The Key of Solomon* in the West.

Luban Xian or Luban Immortal is the patron spirit of, among other things, carpentry, architecture and feng shui.

This may seem a strange origin for a magical grimoire, but before the construction of a house, a temple or a tomb needs intensive occult knowledge drawing on Daoist metaphysics that often find expression through feng shui and magic.

The Luban was jealously guarded by the Chinese Freemasons and feng shui experts with magical leanings for centuries.

To this day an older Chinese generation will speak about the Luban with a kind of hushed whisper coupling both dread and secret admiration.

The Luban seems to preserve very ancient techniques of magic, some of which seems to have originated in the Lushan Mountains in Jiangxi Province.

In the future, the author plans to translate several versions of the Luban into English.

Now the Luban begins with spells to call the fox spirits, so that a kind of contract is made between the Daoist magician and the beings of the fox kingdom. I now give this ritual

translated from the Luban word by word with some annotations to help the reader. This ritual is very powerful and should be done sincerely and properly. Every direction should be followed as there are no shortcuts, especially in rituals like this, which are a serious bond between the sorcerer and the Hu Li family.

The sorcerer should find a quiet place in the countryside or mountains, free from noise and distractions and is suitable to cultivate the practice. Here he will, by certain rituals, meet the Huli spirits in the form of two black and white foxes who will turn into a human shape before his eyes within three to seven days.

On a Fox Moon night the Daoist sets up an altar with a bright oil lamp or candles, sweet incense and a Paiwei or spirit tablet, white wine (shaoju or spirits distilled from maize, chicken breasts, cooked white rice, eggs and salt. The reader should note the dominance of the colour white in this ritual so far. A dish of fruits is also recommended.

Before the altar, he places a new straw mat. For three days before the ritual, the sorcerer should abstain from sex, meat and wine. He should also do careful daily ablutions. The text recommends that the magician also carry a protection talisman this whole time.

While holding the Protect Body Talisman under his tongue he burns two Earth God Talismans (Tudi Fu) and reads the Earth God Spell (Tudi Zhou) seven times.

Next, he takes up the All Immortals Talisman (Zhu Xian Fu) and says the Catch Fox Spell (Ju Hu Zhou) seven times and then burns seven more Earth God Talismans and reads the Earth God Spell seven more times.

It is at this point, says the ancient Luban text, that phenomena begin to occur, such as the magician being pelted with stones and clods of earth. However, the Luban Master tells the sorcerer that he should not show any signs of fear whatsoever.

Instead, take courage and read the Ju Hu Zhou three more times and burn the Command Talisman (Chi Ling Fu).

With persistence, the Fox Spirits appear in human form, sometimes a whole family of them, sometimes male, female and young or old.

The magician then must exclaim to the Foxes that he is a fellow Daoist and not wishing them harm or asking them to do harm but wishes them to find and transport things to him even if they are thousands of miles away, such as Tianshu or Heavenly Books (these are divinely revealed books), magical fungi (Zhi) and herbs, elixirs, money and goods and so forth. He then entreats the Fox Spirits to not leave him, but to assist him in the work of the Dao, in the Way of Perfection. An oath is sworn to seal the contract between the Fox Spirits and the magician.

'Swear that if we should change our hearts, may thunder strike our heads and the eagle claw out our eyes, in adversity, we shall come to assist each other and never to be ungrateful"

With the vow sworn, the magician recites the Immortal Spell and burns one Depart Immortal Talisman (Song Xian Fu).

Whenever the Daoist sorcerer wishes to call the Foxes, he merely needs to set up a quiet room with a bed and a table on which are spread the foods and wine and call Xian Xiong (Brother) or Xian Mei (Immortal Sister). Then with three Calling Immortal Talismans (Zhui Xian Fu) and an Invite Immortal Talisman (Qing Xian Fu) he burns them and says the spell as follows:

O all living beings of Heaven and Earth are a miracle of life, each unique and great with life, we must follow the guidance of our Teachers, Man is a spiritual being, but we are not yet as spiritually powerful as the Immortal Brother and the Immortal Sister, by the cave of the ancient temple or upon the ancient mountain of the Dragon Tower, I invite with a purity of heart that the Great Fox Brother, the Twin Immortal Brother who has attained the Dao, O Immortal Brother, and I call upon you, Great Immortal Sister Fox, Twin Girl Immortal who has attained the Dao, O Celestial Sister, For I have not attained the Dao, Immortal Sister hear me, come, come, quickly, quickly and reveal you're true form, fly here, descend, not merely as in a dream that is vague and uncertain, come in compliance with the Dao Jiao and do not disobey the Law of Heaven, I present this order by Dong Yu Dadi (the Eastern Emperor) Ji Ji Ru Luling!!

Burn the Qing Xian Fu (Invite the Immortal Talisman). If the Huli spirit does not come then burn the Zhui Xian Fu (Pursue the Immortal Talisman). If she still has not made herself manifest then you burn the Chiling Fu (Command Talisman).

The Command Talisman should be consecrated with three points using this spell:

"The first point and Heaven is pure, the Second point and the Earth strikes, the Third point and gods and ghosts are startled for over a thousand miles...."

The sorcerer then reads the astrological power spell:

Lun shui yin yi huo she zhang yue lu xing ri ma liu tu zhang gui jin yang jing shuikai can, shui yuan, zui huo hou bi yue wu ang ri ji wei tu ji, lei jin gou kui mu lang, bi shui huo zhu wei yan xu, ri shu, nu tu, fu niu jin niu ban dou mu jie qi shui gou, wei yan xin yue hu fang ri mian shi tu, yuan jinlong jiao mu jiao wu feng bao da fa shang ji ji ru lu ling!

The Water wheel leads the winged serpent of fire the Moon Deer Star and Solar Horse Willow Earth River Deer Ghost, Metal Sheep Well Water Open Join Water-Monkey Mouth Fire Bi Moon Crow High Sun Rooster

Stomach Earth Rooster like Metal Dog Kui Wood Wolf
Bi Water transports Fire Boar Wei Yan Xu Solar Rat
Woman Earth Bat Ox Metal Ox half, Big Dipper Wood
Jie Qi Water Dog Wei Flaming Heart Moon Fox House
Solar Mian Zhi Earth Origin Metal Dragon Horn Wood
Flood Dragon, I request the Great Treasures of Earth!!
Ji Ji Ru Lu Ling.

Note. This spell is a combination of various terms from Chinese astrology such as the stars, the elements and the 28 Lunar Mansions. The translation is therefore very loose and it will be better to use the Chinese pinyin provided.

The Earth God spell follows next. In Daoist tradition no magic can happen without the permission of the local Earth God, that is Tudi Gong. Tudi Gong is more akin to the animus loci or spirit of a place.

The magician will burn the Tudi Gong Fu and recite the following spell:

O God of this place, Tudi Shen, let your spirit ascend
here from Heaven and Earth and leave the darkness
of the Underworld. I cannot remain at the border. Do
not cease to render great services so that on this day
your name is renowned and purified from above.
Ji Ji Ru Lu Ling.

If the Fox Spirit does not come, burn the Qing Xian Fu (Invite Immortal Talisman) and say the first spell:

"Restrained! Quickly, quickly, quickly descend and
approach, even if you are 800 or a thousand miles away,
I ask you to quickly come, I call out for you to come,
arrive here! LING HONG HONG HONG NAN ZHI
LING I command it by Xinzhou Dragon-Tiger
Mountain Master Patriarch, Zhang Dao Ling, by his
name! Ji Ji Ru Lu Ling!!

If she still does not come, burn the Zhui Xian Fu (Pursue the Immortal Talisman), and read the second spell as follows:

The next spell to follow in Luban's instructions is the spell of Gong Cao Shen. Gong Cao is the envoy of heaven, a kind of Mercury or Hermes in Chinese theology. Burn the Gong Cao Shen Fu then chant:

Gong Cao Shen Spell

O the Three Realms Gong Cao, the Four Duties Messenger, I command you to come to this altar on this day without delay or to risk violating the command of the Court of Heaven!

Again the master burns a Qing Xian Fu and recites the following spell:

One Restraining! Quickly simmer, quickly simmer, quickly simmer, though you are 800 or even a thousand miles away, I ask you to come, quickly come, I call you to come! LING HONG HONG HONG CHA ZHI LING. I request this in the name of the Xinzhou Dragon-Tiger Mountain Master Zhang Dao Ling, JI JI RU LU LING.

If she still refuses to arrive, the Master shall burn the Zhui Xian Fu and say the second spell thus:

Resisting twice, I call you to quickly come and arrive, quickly quickly come even if you are 800 or even a thousand miles away, I invite you to suddenly arrive when I call to you, you do not need to stay away, quickly come in the name of Xinzhou Dragon-Tiger Mountain Master Zhang Dao Ling. JI JI RU LU LING.

He or she then utters the mantra:

PAO LI NA HUN LI KA KA PO CI

Having uttered the two spells, a third follows :

I know the mystery of the waters of the Eastern Sea, polishing the unyielding sword and the halberd, the horsehair bowstring is taut and the sword is unsheathed, quickly come and love me, I invite you to show me your affection and kindness, OM LI HONG, OMI LI HONG, OM LI HONG, By command of Zhang Dao Ling, Master of the Xinzhou Dragon-Tiger Mountain. JI JI RU LU LING!

The magician utters a final spell called the San Ju or Three Sentences:

The Primordial Chaos (Hundun) at the beginning of time divided, the vast unknown Great Void (Taixu) gave birth to Destiny, I request the spirit to come, to speak, to come! Ji Ji Ru Lu Ling!

SUI LI HONG, ZA LI PAN, PAO LI JIAN, HONG HONG OM, OM LI HONG, YI

When the fox arrives she may not be in human form, remarks the instructions of the Luban, therefore the sorcerer must read the Transform into Human Form Spell (Bianhua Renxing Zhou) and burn the Transformation Talisman (Bianhua Fu). The spell reads thus:

O I request that on this day, that you descend to this altar and change your form to that of a human, and that between I and you, there will be a great attachment and affection, a love and a friendship, by the treasured name of the Jade Emperor's command, quickly transform, I command it by Xinzhou Dragon-Tiger MountainMaster Zhang Dao Ling, Ji Ji Ru Lu Ling!!!

The magician now in contact with the Fox Spirit forms a

bond with her can now burn a Depart Immortal Talisman (Song Xian Fu) and read the Depart Immortal Spell three times:

> Spirit of Heaven, Spirit of Earth, cut the bamboo, break the enchantment, disperse and begone evil spirits, white-faced ones leave this house, I request it by command of the Xinzhou Dragon-Tiger Mountain Master, Zhang Dao Ling! Ji Ji Ru Lu Ling!!

If you do not burn the Song Xian Talisman, then you can say the above Depart Immortal Spell seven times and then repeat the Spell:

> The Primordial Chaos (Hundun) at the beginning of time divided, the vast unknown Great Void (Taixu) gave birth to Destiny, I request the spirit to come, to speak, to come! Ji Ji Ru Lu Ling!

SUI LI HONG, ZA LI PAN, PAO LI JIAN, HONG HONG OM, OM LI HONG, YI

This spell has many interesting aspects to it and is essentially a crash course in the Daoist methodology of evoking spirits.

The authority invoked for example is Zhang Dao Ling, perhaps the key figure in organising Magical and religious Daoism

Master Zhang Dao Ling was the founder of the Way of the Celestial Masters. In 142AD Master Zhang experienced in ecstasy a vision of Taishang Laojun, the eternal and immortal form of Lao Zi, and from that moment organised Magical Taoism began.

Zhang Dao Ling himself became immortal and is frequently invoked in Taoist rituals, including this one.

The use of mantras is also interesting. Hong is the Chinese equivalent of the seed syllable HUM or HUNG, a powerful seed syllable in Tantric practice. It has long been associated with powerful protection.

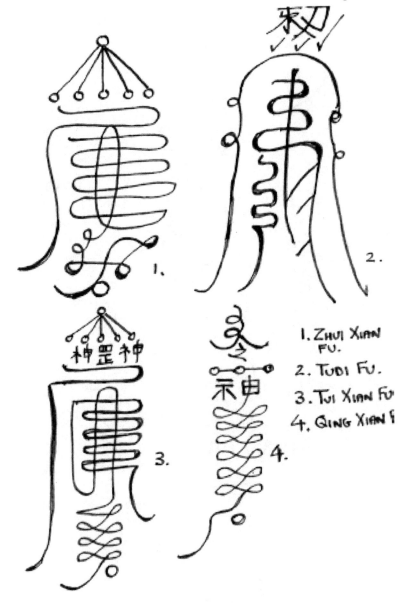

1. Zhui Xian Fu.
2. Tudi Fu.
3. Tui Xian Fu
4. Qing Xian F

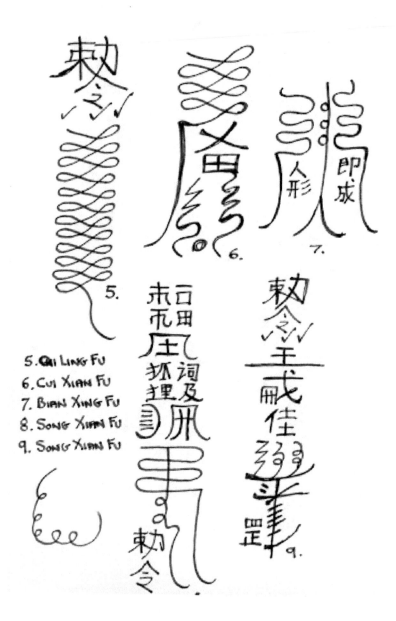

5. QI LING FU
6. CUI XIAN FU
7. BIAN XING FU
8. SONG XIAN FU
9. SONG XIAN FU

How to do the Nine Tail Fox Immortal Sincerity Ritual

Before entering the deeper mysteries of the Fox Fairy it is recommended that the aspirant devote him or herself to the Sincerity Test of 100 Days. In Chinese magic, just because a person wants to work with or feels pulled towards a spirit doesn't mean they want to work with you! Like any relationship you have to take it slowly and prove that you are sincere, hence the sincerity test. If you cannot even find the time and means to light a stick of incense and say a few words daily to Hu Xian, there is cause to doubt your aspiration. It is rather like entering a new relationship. You don't jump in guns blazing and making demands and automatically assume you have a right to invoke her. You earn it.

For 100 days, you do the sincerity rite and nothing else to contact the Nine Tail Fox Spirit.

From ancient shamanism arose the far-reaching and yet secretive cult of the Fox Immortal. Very few, in reality, know it. Evolving in the wild forests and mountains of North-East China in the Beima schools of animal totem spirits where the powerful Fox family ruled over even the tiger, snake, bird, wolf and other deities, the Fox School reached as far as Korea, Japan and Thailand. The Fox is one of the personal teachers of the members of our school.

Interestingly and perhaps not coincidentally, Hu Xian was the chief totem and rumoured mother of the founder of Japanese Onmyodo.

One of the noted characteristics of the disciples of the Fox is that they are fascinating. They have a certain something. I could name a few well known Hong Kong stars who are devotees. But in all probability, the HK fox cult is a bit of a money scam.

You could compare the fox aura to the Celtic idea of fairy glamour and the idea of the binding gaze ... Fascination. While in the West it's seen as evil, the *meitong* or bewitching eye in fox society is about enchanting in a less cursing and more captivating way. Neither does it mean being loud and forceful. The fox's charisma is deep and brooding, not being a loud obnoxious jerk lol.

There are several meditations used, but it's all useless without the correct linking by the ancient ritual.

For the first time in English, here is how you begin.

1. The Dizi (disciple) obtains a picture or statue of Jiuwei Hu Xian, the Nine-Tailed Fox Immortal. Yellow or white is best. Do not use images of Hu San Taiye (Fox Grandfather) or Hu San Tainai (Fox Auntie).
    Put it on the altar.
    For 100 days do nothing but offer One incense stick each day and request the following invocation:

    I the disciple respectfully welcome and call you O Fox Immortal, blessed Immortal, who I long for over a thousand miles. I the disciple offer incense every day that you may kindly assist me O Blessed Lady. In the hope that the Virtuous Law is accomplished and the disciple is ten thousand times fortunate. My heart is true. Your disciple is willing.

2. After 100 days of the 'sincerity test' increase the offering to three incense sticks and red fruits such as red cherries, red dates, longans and red flowers. Now offer three pillars of incense. The prayer changes:

    I the disciple courteously call you O Fox Immortal to descend today. I am sincere and my heart is devoted and aches for you. O great Fox Immortal goddess, give me the disciple, the Immortal Way, open my spiritual doors and purify and open my eyes. I shall give you daily offerings and incense continually! The disciple gives a hundred thanks!

Write your name and year, month, day and hour of birth on red paper and put it under the incense burner.

You should also have a bowl decorated with a red floral design, filled with water and placed before the incense burner.

Leave overnight so the water is 'touched' by Hu Xian. It becomes Jade Wine.

On waking, wash your face and anoint your eyes.

In 100 days, fascinating eyes, more youthful and attractive. Fortune in social and romance occurs via the Peach Blossom gate.

Over time more mysteries are imparted ... She will teach her witchcraft and alchemy.

The Rituals And Magic Of The Nine Tail Fox Girl Of Dragon-Tiger Mountain

In an earlier chapter, we learned that in China the central focus of the devotion and practice of the Nine Tail Fox Girl was and still is the Immortal Fox Temple at the Dragon-Tiger Mountain Temple complex in the south-eastern Province of Jiangxi. Dragon-Tiger Mountain is the spiritual root of all Taoist magic as it was the chief temple of Zhang Dao Ling. It was Zhang Dao Ling who recruited and formed a contract with the spiritual kingdom of Hu Li Jing.

What follows is the 'official' spiritual practice and service of the Nine Tail Fox lady as given by the Hall of the Foxes Temple on Dragon-Tiger Mountain.

Ideally, so say the texts, you would have gone to Dragon-Tiger Mountain's Fox Hall and yourself obtained ashes from the censer upon her altar.

You would take these ashes home and add them to your censer thus transporting the power to begin a new Master Thurible (Zhu Lu or Host God Incense Burner).

The home fox altar should consist of a medium-sized flat table draped with a red cloth. At the head of the altar should be an image of Jiu Wei Hu Xian Niang Niang, (Lady Nine Tail Fox Immortal/Fairy). This can be a picture or a statue. Do not use anything too sexually provocative. I mention this as many images have come from Thailand that, though they can be used for other forms of magical practice, cannot be for this devotional and yes, even initiatory and magical practice.

An ideal image of the Nine Tail Fox Girl is a beautiful Chinese girl with her hair bound up in the style of a classical Chinese lady of classical China and wearing a white robe to indicate the mysteries of death. And yet her sensual curves are hinted at beneath the white silk, to indicate the mysteries of eros. Her nine tails are around her. Her skin is pale and her face is beautiful and yet regal.

You will want two red candles on either side.

A bell.

A platter for offerings of fruit. (red fruits are the best, but it is not essential)

A vase for flowers, red ones are preferred but white is also ok.

A cup for offering tea or wine.

The censer can be a beautiful bronze urn or as simple as a porcelain bowl. Either way, it should be filled with rice and salt, with a few dried beans thrown in. Arrange three Chinese coins in a triangle on top of the rice. When inserting the three incense sticks, put them through the holes in the coins.

The coins represent the power and unity of Heaven (round) and Earth (square hole), and three to represent the Three Primary Powers of the Tao. These three powers manifest in many ways ... Yin, Yang and Dao; Heaven, Earth and Man; the San Qing or Three Pure Ones, and the San Bao or Three Treasures of Man ... Jing, Qi and Shen. We will learn more about these powers in people later in discussing internal alchemy as it pertains to the Fox Immortal Tradition.

It would be ideal if the Altar has a Da Fu or Great Talisman. This is a large poster-sized talisman or tablet which is like the 'engine and battery' of the Altar. Essentially it stores the power of all rituals conducted at the altar. This can be painted on a stiff card or on wood. The field must be red and use black lettering for the characters. The tablet essentially lists the names of various deities and spirits that can be called and invoked by the Fox magician. Due to its complexity, you may not want to use this at the beginning of your practices but it is highly recommended that you do it at a later stage. You will find the power increases a thousandfold and more magical resources are open to the practitioner. I will detail this in a separate section because, as I just noted, it is a fairly complex piece of magic.

In Taoist magic we orientate our altars to the Northern cardinal point, meaning that in your room, you want the altar in the northern section. The North for us is the place of power where spiritual, life and occult forces are injected into our reality, so to speak.

Having set up the altar, the magician can proceed with the ritual. The ritual text is known as the Huxian Jinke Yulu Zhenjiang or the Fox Fairy Golden Rules and True Precepts Classic.

The magician approaches the altar in darkness. He first lights the two red candles proclaiming the light Candle spell:

> The candle is lit and in the eight directions, the light brightly shines. All the evil spirits and demons are defeated and cannot be concealed within the Earth.

Next follows the Fox Fairy Incense Spell, the magus lighting the three or nine incense sticks.

> Cultivating diligently in the Yungtai Cave, Dragon-Tiger Mountain is the seat of power, here there is freedom, verdant with pines and cypress the Imperial Palace is concealed, the peoples of the moonlight altar ceremony come to present incense to you O Fox Fairy!

The light and the incense are now lit. Note that the incense should never be sandalwood, when offered to the Fox Girl, it should be of a heavy, sensuous nature. The ideal incense for Hu Xian is agarwood. Also, note that incense offered should always be in odd numbers and never even.

Now the censer wafts clouds of incense to communicate with the spirits and there is light, the celebrant must now purify himself. The next few spells are common to all Taoist rituals and not unique to the Fox Rites.

Firstly, the spell of Purifying the Heart, that is, to clean the mind.

> The Great Star rises. Regardless of troubles, it is stable, exorcising and binding the evil ones, protecting life and body. There arises wisdom and clarity. The mind is at peace. The Three Hun Souls are eternal and thus there is no sadness.

Next, the magician purifies the mouth or speech. In Daoist belief, the voice is a powerful magical tool that can express the purified and magical mind, but before this can really gel, the magician must consciously activate that function. Hence the Jing Kou Zhou or Purify the Mouth/Speech Spell:

> O Dan Zhu (Red Cinnabar), Lord of the mouth, expels the poisonous miasma, She Shen, Lord of my Tongue is righteous.
> Opening life and accomplishing Spirit, the Thousand Toothed God drives away evil influences and defends me. The Tiger Throat Lord of the East induces saliva, the Heart-Mind Lord, Cinnabar Essence orders me, opens the true thought stream of spirit, refining the liquid. The Tao is Eternal!!

The Purify Speech Spell has some interesting points. It recalls extremely ancient practices whereby the body is considered to be filled with many spirits or gods, all cooperating to sustain, protect and even evolve the human condition. The sages of Taoism taught that the master can communicate with his own body and bring it to perfection and even tease out certain remarkable abilities. The mouth spirit is envisioned as Red

Cinnabar for example. The spell then goes on to communicate with the spirits of the tongue, teeth and throat. Those who are familiar with Taoist cultivation will know that all parts of the mouth are vital tools in alchemy. The Tongue is considered a bridge between the lower body and the higher psychic centres of the head, and for this reason, the tongue is placed in certain parts of the palate, but usually behind the teeth. The tongue itself is considered to be a literal 'tongue of flame' and connected with fire and the heart's energetic complex. The teeth are often tapped in alchemical exercises for a certain amount of time.

Saliva, though it may seem odd to some readers, is, in Taoist magic, a medium that can catch certain essences of an occult nature. When saliva is made in this way we refer to it as Jade Fluid or Jade Wine.

With a purified mind and purified speech, the master of the Fox Temple must now cleanse the body.

Lingbao Tianzun comforts the body of the disciple. The Hun and Po souls, the Five Internal Organs, and the Mysterious Underworld and the Green Dragon, the White Tiger assemble with their weapons, and the Vermillion Bird and Dark Warrior all guard my body!

This is quite straightforward. The magician invokes Lingbao Tianzun, one of the Three Pure Ones who separated all things into Yin and Yang.

The Five Internal organs are the heart, liver, lungs, kidneys and spleen and these correspond to the Five Elements of Chinese philosophy.

Finally, the magus invokes the Four Auspicious beasts who rule over the Four Directions and four out of five of the elements.

The Green Dragon is Wood and the liver and is to the East of the celebrant.

The White Tiger is Metal and the lungs and is to the West.

The Vermillion Bird is Fire and the Heart and is to the South.

The Northern Warrior (sometimes shown as a black turtle) is to the North and corresponds to Water and the kidneys.

Having prepared the self and is duly protected and empowered, the Fox Magician must now purify the Altar.

Purifying the Altar is a necessary process in working with any spiritual forces in Daoist magic. As the cliche goes, when you activate magical tools a kind of beacon is lit that signals to the spiritual world that you are open for business. Though you may succeed in calling the beings you wish for you will also attract those that are undesirable. Such spirits, according to the teachings of Daoism. can be lesser nature spirits or lonely ghosts who have a predisposition to feed on energy wherever it is available. Besides these factors, your altar may have been left unattended for a day or two and it will likely have picked up some psychic detritus. This is inevitable. Thus the altar must be cleansed regularly.

The magician is advised to obtain some gold spirit money, and wipe down the altar and then burn the paper. He or she can also use water that has been previously blessed and then take some in the mouth and spray it over the altar. The water should not be spat out in a stream but by building up pressure in the mouth, it can be turned into thousands of cloud-like droplets that can be sprayed in a mist-like form.

The spell of cleansing the altar is as follows:

Taishang strikes the Golden Bell (ring the bell) and it resounds with jadelike sounds, one hundred fig trees conceal the land, a crowd of fierce spirits guard the high forest (Qian Lin), Heavenly flowers are distributed like rain, the drums beat excitedly. The tranquillity of heaven is unsurpassed.

The Golden Boy dances and plays the Jade Lute. Eight rays of sunlight enter therein, the heart is compliant to the fundamental laws of the Dao, and Guo and Yi serve the Five Profound Voices.

The cleansing with the gold spirit paper can be done before the spell is said. The spell itself is a highly esoteric piece of writing, too complex to go into here. However, the more experienced Daoist may well notice that it references the internal landscape of the alchemical body of man.

Nothing in Daoist magic can be made manifest without the permission and power of the land on which we stand. The magician with his eyes and heart turned towards heaven will often forget the power of the ground beneath his feet. So in the teachings of the Chinese sages, before anything can be done we call upon the Earth spirits to aid us and to open the gates of manifestation. In practical terms, this means our local 'Tudi'. Tudi is often translated as Landlord God, but a closer idea is the *genii loci*, the Spirit of a Place. Without the aid of the Tudi, not a lot will happen magically in the realm of Earth.

Tudi is usually, and for convenience, envisioned as a kindly and bearded old man in simple clothes. It is of course tempting to compare it with western envisionings of the Earth Spirit as a gnome, kobold etc.

The Spell of Land Purifying thus follows:

The origins of peace and tranquillity are thus declared. Ten thousand spirits of the mountains, the True Official of the Land, Spirit of the Earth. O spirits assemble in the east and assemble in the west. The grain must not be startled, let it return on the correct path. Let every direction be purified so that all directions are at peace. The Altar Room is guarded. Taishang possesses the essence of life, catching the evil spirits, The Divine King is guardian, defending us by chanting the sutras and converting all beings to the true path. YUAN HENG LI ZHEN.

Again the invocation is quite straightforward, a calling to the spirits of the land and mountains. Some of those spirits might well be 'wild' so they are recruited to the cause of the Dao. The magician should not worry if he happens not to live by any mountains! The mountains of our world have incredible power that makes its way through the telluric network of our planet. A magician in the Thames Valley for example can invoke the powers of the Five Sacred Mountains of China.

The final invocation of Yuan Heng Li Zhen is pregnant with meaning and is a powerful vibratory mantra in its own right. It is usually translated as 'from the source, creating success, constancy bears fruit'. It is the first four characters of the I Ching, and every description of the hexagrams in that august tome have it in some form or another.

Now the Spell Of Cleansing Heaven And Earth follows on from the Spell of Purifying the Earth. We have invoked and pacified the spirits of the earth and have their permission and have recruited them to our cause. Now we call on the two fundamental powers of Chinese metaphysics, that of Tian or Heaven and that of Earth or Di. The two are the great poles and the Yin and Yang of manifested existence.

> Heaven and Earth are free from affliction. Qi energy
> disperses from the central cave of the Profound
> Mystery, dazzling Light, highest origin.
> The Gods of the Eight Directions send me the calmness
> of the Lingbao Talisman whose name informs the
> Highest Heavens. Qian receives it. The Cave of the
> Highest Mystery slays the demonic and binds the evil
> influences and thousands of ghosts are destroyed. The
> Spell of the Central Mountain God, the Origin of the
> Jade Character is grasped and recited continually!!

The next part of the standard ritual is quite obvious. With incense the lit incense sticks in both hands in a prayer hand posture, he says the following spell.

Spell Of The Offering Of Incense

The Tao is learned in the heart,
And the incense is the vehicle of the heart,
The incense, O how it warms the Jade Urn,
O the heart comes before the Emperor,
The True Immortal looks down from above,
The banner of the Immortal signals the arrival of the heavenly chariot,
And so the reports of mankind are closed,
We directly communicate with the Nine Heavens.
Quickly by the Law!!!

On completion, he inserts the joss sticks into the censer.

The Golden Light Spell

The Golden Light Spell is one of the most important and fundamental practices of magical Daoism. One of my western magical friends once described it as the Middle Pillar on steroids!

The Golden light is powerful enough that in seasoned practitioners its radiance shows up in photographs. It is best at this point to cut to the chase and learn it step by step. Even when not conducting rituals, it is highly recommended that the Daoist magician practices this daily.

1. Let the Dizi sit in his chosen position or stand in his chosen stance. Adopt natural breath.

2. Interlace all the fingers. Let the little fingers stand erect and touch at the tips. Do the same with the index fingers. Then let the thumb tips touch but they point down. The ring and middle fingers remain interlaced to form a 'platform'. (see diagram}.

3. Raise the hands so the tips of the thumbs are at the level of the *niwan* (third eye).

4. Chant the spell as follows. Note I have given the spell both in English and Pinyin Mandarin Chinese. You can use either, though purists may prefer the Chinese version. Since this is a spell, the sounds themselves aren't magical but the word-image formation is. Only actual mantric sounds will remain untranslated.

5. As you read the spell you must visualise the Seal of the Golden Light above your head. It is a fairly complex structure so I would suggest drawing it out a few times to understand the structure, and for the first few practices. Have it drawn on a card. The seal must be in bright golden light and pulsing with humming and oscillating waves of golden vibrancy. Bright, luminous, powerful.

6. O Heaven, the profound One origin of All,
We cultivate, spiralling through countless Kalpas.
To attain transcendence.
Inside and outside the three realms.
The Tao is the honoured One,
O the Seal of Golden Light,
Covers and protects my body,
It cannot be seen,
It cannot be heard,
Encompassing the entire Universe,
Nurturing all beings.
By One Enchantment,
My body radiates the Light,
Protected in the Three Realms,
The Five Emperors welcome me!
Homage is paid by a thousand Gods,
The Thunder is invoked!!
Ghosts are terrified, the evil ones tremble,
The disintegration of monstrous shapes,
Power is produced from within.
Overseen by the Mighty Lords of Thunder,
Wisdom and magical skill blend.

The Five Forms of Qi shine with life.
The Golden Light instantly erupts into being,
By the Logos of the Jade Emperor,
Quickly by the command of the Law !!!!

Tian di Xuan Zong,
Wan qi ben gen,
Guang xiu wan Jie,
Zheng wu shen tong,
San Jie nei wai,
Wei Dao du zun,
Fu you jin guan,
Zhao hu wu shen,
Shi Zhi bu Jian,
Ting Zhi bu wen,
Boa Luo tian di,
Yang yu qun sheng,
Shou chi gi hian,
Shen you Guang ming,
San Jie Shi Wei,
Wu-di si ying,
Wan shen Chao li,
Yi Shi Lei ting,
Gui yan sang dan jing,
Guai wang xing'
Nei you pi li,
Lei Shen yin ming,
Tong hui jiao che,
Wu qi teng teng,
Jin Guang su xian,
Fu fu Zhen ren.
JI Ji Ru Luling!!!

7. Now still at brow level, let the hands separate. The hands sweep slowly down in arcs to the sides of the body. As you do this, envision a trail of golden light that forms an Auric egg of golden light that is seen to cover your whole body like a forcefield.

It is a kind of energy field that can be envisioned as a golden egg that dark entities fizzle out upon if they come into contact with it, rather like one of those UV insect killer lamps you sometimes see in restaurants.

Later when you are confident, you can begin internally storing the golden light in the *dantian* and even practice channelling it through the hands for healing purposes. Using the Sword Mudra (which see later) you can shoot negative entities

Mudra of the Golden Light

as if you possess some kind of psychic laser blaster.

Practice consistently at least three to four times a week.

The final preparatory spell is the Spell of the Mysterious Gathering or Spell of the Profound Mystery as it is sometimes called. It is a call to the Court of Heaven and the assembly of the honoured Gods and Immortals.

Spell Of The Mysterious Gathering

The Cloud Seal of the Mysterious Void,
Has been since the beginning of the Great Kalpa,
Suddenly it is near and suddenly it is far,
Sometimes sinking and sometimes floating,
Moving to and fro in the Five Directions,
Of the assembly of numerous Masters,
The True Emperor of Heaven,
He takes up his brush to write in the Book,
To reveal the Seal of the Cave,
And the Book of Talismans,
The Primal Cause descends,
With courage teaching the true words,
Illuminating when being,
Obscuring when not,
Serious ills are self-healed,
The strength of those suffering in work and the dust
of the Earth,
Assisting those who are imprisoned in desire,
Bringing the gift of ascension into the Realm of the
Immortals.
Quickly by the Law!!!!

Having finished all the spells of preparation it is now time to call the actual Hu Xian, the Immortal Fox Spirits.

There are a number of them all with different functions

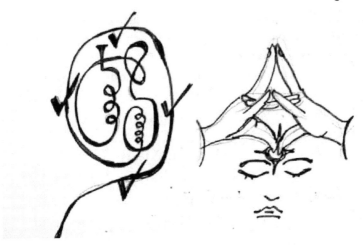

Golden Light Seal and hand seal.
Thumbs are positioned over the 'third eye'

Position of Golden Light Spell

and attributes who work with different aspects of Fox Magic. Some are designated by their colours which are attributed to the Five Elements /Planets of Chinese philosophy. On an individual basis, you can work with any one of them outside the confines of this ritual for a particular purpose. Within this ritual, they are all called upon in the manner of a court assembly.

1. Huang Hu Xian
Yellow Fox Fairy

O Yellow Fox Fairy, Immortal and honoured Lady, please come to this altar and be seated. By her hand seal, she leads the warriors to slay evil demons. The Heavenly Teacher bestows the Lingpai upon me, the command of the Celestial Troops, and so they follow my orders, marching with their swords and thus ghosts and evil influences are defeated, and so black magicians and evil masters are defeated and slain by the sword.

Celestial lady, high and great, you command the Celestial Troops and protect the nation and expand the Daoist Way in a thousand li in all directions.

The Yellow Fox Fairy is associated with the Central direction and the element of Earth. As you can see from the invocation, she is a highly protective and powerful warrior who can be invoked against black magic.

Next follows the White Fox Fairy who is associated with who is the classic Nine Tail Fox Fairy and is here elementally associated with Metal and the direction of the West. She is invoked to clear obstacles and potential impurities in the disciple's immediate environment.

2.Bai Hu Xian
White Fox Fairy

Lady White Fox appears, floating on the clouds, coming

to us from the remotest ends of the Earth, Nine Tail Fox, blessings from Heaven, auspicious and generous, returning to Earth to give peace to the people, appear to me, she who gives inner joy, touches me O Mysterious One. I give you honour and devotion, bless us and make our space healthy and give us vitality, make me popular among the people and give abundance!

3. Xuan Hu Xian
The Dark Or Black Fox Fairy

The Dark Fox Fairy is associated with the element of Water and the North. She is especially called upon in matters of commerce and finance and other matters where the flow of money and riches are concerned. Note that in Chinese occultism money and its flow are associated with a continuity that flows from the wellspring of the ancestors.

All over the mountain the peonies blossom, O Princess of riches the luxuriant petals flourish from generation to generation, the Dark Fox Immortal sits in the centre holding the precious jar of wine, and the good people and merchants come to pay her devotion. The golden treasures of Kings are open to the people. The hidden treasures of the family are indicated by the Big Dipper.

The land under heaven is mastered by spreading the Dao!!

4. Hong Hu Xian
The Red Fox Fairy

The Red Fox Fairy is associated with the South and the element of Fire. Passion, love, sexuality and fertility are among her gifts. Note that the peach blossom is the symbol of sexual love and romance in Daoist magic. That branch of magic associated with love and sexuality is known as the Peach Blossom Branch.

> O the peach blossoms open, for a thousand li the scent of their blossoms float in the air, the happy fate of lovers descends from Heaven. The flowers open and bear fruit for the Nine Tail Red Fox is here. The Incense coils upwards and there is golden light.

5.Hehe Hu Xian
Harmonising Fox Fairy

Hehe is a Chinese term that implies harmony and marriage of two things in perfect accord and sympathy. In Daoist magic, Hehe spells are used to improve relationships and heal divisions in marriages or other partnerships.

> Harmonious Fox Fairy, you are beautiful, the disciples burn incense and bow to you and we request light to descend like a mist on the mountain top. Inside the cave, peach flowers blossom.
>
> Whoever sees me shall like me. Happy marriage, the peach flowers are precious and illuminate the happy fate that brings lovers together, causing a thousand predestined lovers to link hands, the husband and wife remain together for a thousand years, reaching harmony.

6. Lan Hu Xian, The Blue Fox Fairy

The Blue Fox Fairy is associated with the East and Wood. She is powerful as a destroyer of demons. As the vicegerent of wood and Jupiter, she is wonderful to invoke not only for exorcism of evil spirits but for growth and beginning new projects.

On the Mountain of Cloud and Mist, displaying mighty

magical powers. The Blue Nine Tail Fox sits in the midst, a sound rises to the Heavens and suddenly the Earth shakes and demons and ghosts pass away and disintegrate. Heavenly time passes by in the Heavens above. The Earth hides us from the evil star, All are at peace wherever they go and are free from disease, protected from calamity and in good health!

7. Qing Qiu Huxian
Green Hill Fox Fairy

The Green Hill Fox Fairy is a master of song and dance and can entrance people thereby. Therefore she is popularly invoked by musicians and entertainers as well as public speakers, writers and poets in need of eloquence. She is both a muse and an enchantress.

On the Green Hill Mountain she lightly treads and sings and chants, Under the Moon dancing with grace like a celestial maiden, Ten thousand people gather to hear her play the zither (fuqin), A gathering of guests listen to the fairy melodies.

8. Xue Hu Xian. Snow Fox Fairy

Another class of well-known spells are the Snow Mountain spells. These are mainly used in healing, the coldness for example used to cure fevers. The orchid mentioned is Dendrobium Nobile, a plant that can flower in the winter with a beautiful bloom. It is one of the fundamental fifty plants of Chinese medicine.

On the cloudy summit is Snow Fox Fairy, today she plucks the sword leaved orchid and sings of the dew in the night, The noble orchid water method when poured brings calm and peace, Exorcising all diseases and ailments until they are removed,

Wearing the Cloud Talisman the unhealthy ghosts are kept at bay, One incantation of the spell and the gods and ghosts are startled, Protecting the home, safe and sound, the house, the road, the village has everlasting tranquillity.

9. Ruyi Huxian
Wish-fulfilling Fox Fairy

The ninth Fox Fairy is Ruyi, which can be translated as the gratifying or wish-fulfilling fox. She satisfies the wishes of the devotee. Ruyi is also the name of a ritual tool in Taoism which confers good fortune and blessing.

I request the Fox Fairy of Great Divine Power,
Awe-inspiring strength and power of Heaven and Earth,
On your head, you wear the magnificent Light of the Dao,
You wear a long red robe of the Dao,
In your hand, you hold manifold wishes,
Wishes become true and real,
The Sword emitting red rays for ten thousand years,
The wish stops the evil ones and the flash of lightning protects the family home.

Next follows a general spell to the Nine Tail Fox Fairy:

Spell Of
The Nine Tail Fox Fairy

The Nine-Tailed Fox descends from the Heavens, Bringing good fortune and security to all the people of Earth, Bringing assistance and aid to ever-changing circumstances of the disciple,

Evil spirits and ghosts are defeated in the womb of the Earth, There are ten thousand Celestial beings in the many branches of the Law,

Ten million support me in the application of the law and the Daoist Rites shall manifest their power!!

Spirit Of The Kingdom
Of Dreams Spell

This spell, though part of the ritual as a whole can like most of the spells here be used by disciples to dream walk or astrally travel to the home of the Fox Fairy to commune with her and perhaps have questions answered and teachings were given, Note this shouldn't be confused with Western-style 'pathworkings' or creative visualisation. It should manifest as a literal flying soul experience, not a vague imaginary exercise.

In the vast Heavens are untold pleasures within,

O vast is the world of mankind,

A cool breeze comes,

On the clouds we walk,

Walking in the clouds are the Immortals who have attained the Dao,

And so the Fox Fairy is in the remotest Mountains,

Show us the path to the Mountain of the Dao,

Within the Cave we ask,

The Hun Soul flies ten million miles,

To the Mysterious place to learn.

Mount Tu Family Fox Fairy Girl Of
Extraordinary Beauty

This is a lesser-known manifestation of the Fox Fairy that is and was peculiar to Tushan or Tu Mountain in Chongqing in Jiangsu. This was the home of among others the ancestral and legendary Shaman-King, Yu the Great.

> O the Tushan Clan Girl is beautiful,
> The Nine-Tailed Fox is auspicious and brings great prosperity,
> Poems and songs arise from a chorus in the wind and clouds,
> Ten million children and grandchildren follow you,
> East, West, South and North and Centre,
> You are the Mother of generations of Kings O Immortal Mother.

Thus goes the main body of the Ritual, which needs to be cultivated at least weekly or monthly over time.

In this way the Taoist devotee experiences communion with and the numinous power of the Fox Maidens.

At certain times, the practitioner may choose to work with one form of the Maiden, for example in times of financial need or when beginning a business he may call upon the Black Fox Maiden. Hehe, Fox Maiden may help in marriage and relationship problems, and Peach Blossom (love/erotic) spells.

I leave it up to the ingenium of the practitioner.

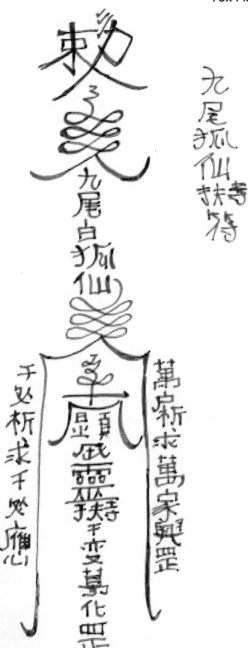

Talisman used in the Temple of the Fox. On yellow paper with black ink.
Stick to the altar edge.

The Forbidden Tantra
Of The Fox Girl

Several hundred years ago the Japanese Buddhist community was left reeling from the uncovering of a cult in their midst. The rumours were of a secret cult with the Fox Dakini at its head. Its secret rituals involved sex and necromantic rituals with skulls emulating the powers of the Fox Spirits who used skulls in their transformation rituals.

It may sound like a cheap newspaper exposé or reminiscent of the Satanic Panic 'revelations' of the 1980s, but it was true and the name of the school or Ryu involved was the Tachikawa Ryu.

Sources claim that the school was founded in 1113 by the unorthodox monk Nikan, but by the 14th century had been branded a heresy and rooted out of Japanese Shingon and Esoteric Buddhist culture (mikkyo).

Like all tantras, its basic aim was the transformation of human consciousness beyond the limits of ordinary perception. In the case of the Tachikawa, sexual energy or jing was the key tool used towards this end. Furthermore, the Tachikawa disciple would employ techniques of magic and necromancy, such as the use of the skull to obtain siddhis (occult powers) and a kind of familiar that can give oracles and the like.

The School of Tachikawa had as its fundamental basis the teaching that all phenomena exist in polarity, a fundamental teaching in both Tantra and Daoism. Tachikawa seems to have blended the two streams of thought into one teaching under the direction of Dakini Ten, the great Fox Dakini.

Dakini Ten was often dreaded by the classical Japanese as a

being who vampirised the 'yellow' of men to sustain her own life. Obviously, the nature of this mysterious 'yellow' that was the food of the fox maiden was sexual energy or jing.

Yet 'yellow' is also the basis of liberation and immortality in both Daoist and tantric yoga-based systems.

Both in yoga and Taoism, the raw sexual energies are the raw prima materia of all kinds of wonderful transmutations that lead to ecstatic states of consciousness, magical abilities, but most importantly, the creation of an immortal body. This is not in any way a physical immortal body but a spiritual body that is capable of transcending the forces of death themselves. This tradition is hinted at by practically every tradition, even as far as the Greek mysteries.

In the Dharma of the Fox, it is taught that sexual energies are a double-edged sword that can lead to ruin or attainment. We saw how in the folk tales the Fox Maiden can feast on the sexual jing of a man to sustain and fuel her evolution towards the ultimate goal of immortality. However, it is equally taught to the worthy that those same processes can be utilised by human devotees of the Fox Immortal to catapult consciousness into new realms of bliss and ecstasy as well as develop the immortal body.

Tachikawa taught that all phenomena manifest in male and female polarities. We can term them Yin and Yang, Heaven and Earth, God and Goddess and in Shingon terminology, the Womb Realm (feminine) and the Diamond Vajra Realm (male).

The chief essence of the Tachikawa teaching was ' To be united as man and woman is to be united with the Buddha'.

In the tantric yoga of the Tachikawa, the idea was to unite polarities in such perfect equilibrium as to transcend duality and enter into a state of the Absolute. My Qabalistic readers may understand this through the idea of uniting perfect Love and Wisdom to attain the oneness of Kether, the Crown.

Engaging in this tantra is a difficult and long process that begins at midnight and ends at the first glimmer of the rising sun at dawn.

The couple must first bathe together in a hot spring, say the original texts but without making any physical contact. They can enjoy the sight of each other and so heighten the erotic energies through unrequited sexual longing.

A small clean and spotless temple room is arranged. In the room is an altar with the image of Dakini Ten upon it, an incense burner, flowers and other seasonal offerings of nature. There are five candles of five colours to represent the five elements.

North. Black. Water.
South. Red. Fire.
East. Green or Blue. Wood.
West. White. Metal.
Centre. Yellow. Earth.

The incense and candles are lit.
The man says:
'I aspire to enter the Womb Realm'.
The woman says:
'I aspire to receive the Diamond Thunderbolt'.

A comfortable mattress or seat is arranged in the Southwest.

At the stroke of midnight, the man sits cross-legged or in some other posture that is comfortable to him. He should be erect. The woman slides down his shaft so they are joined, diamond vajra to the red lotus of the Womb Realm. They do not thrust or attempt to 'have sex'.

They harmonise their breath with the mantra A-HUM or A-HUNG.

A is on the inhalation and represents the feminine Yin component, the HUNG part is the masculine, yang part. Using the mantra they synchronise their breaths to become one organism vibrating to the same rhythm.

They must now blend their five elements.

First, they focus on breathing in Green Qi of Wood

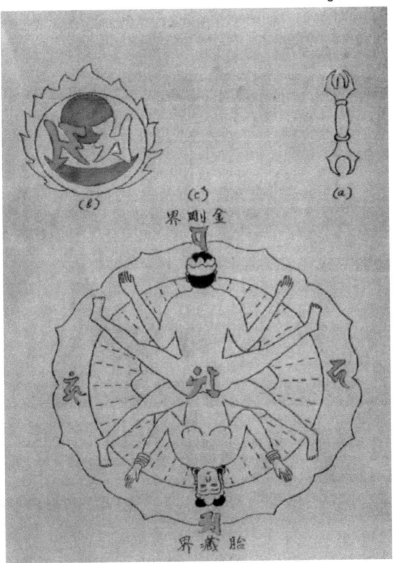

Form of the Tantric Rite of the Tachikawa with Ah Hung Syllable.

simultaneously and merge them, flowing through both of their bodies. Then continue with the red of fire, the black of water, the white of metal and the yellow of earth. Around themselves, they create a rainbow of the five colours. They remain in this tantric union until dawn. At this point, a spontaneous mutual orgasm is permitted that will cast them into a state of consciousness that exists in perfect equilibrium of polarities and the elements. They taste the bliss of ecstasy.

Six hours is a long time to remain in this posture, so there is, arguably, some hyperbole in the above account and one may need to make adjustments or use common sense and intuition to make it work for you. The process in itself is utter simplicity but very difficult to engage in, but those who will and dare will no doubt report many wonders.

The second mystery of the Tachikawa cult was far more shocking to Japanese society. In many ways this was the culmination of the total mysteries of the Fox, both sex and death were made to serve the will of the magician.

For this ritual, the tantric magician needed to obtain a skull. Sometimes an animal skull was sufficient but most practitioners obtained a human skull. You might note that we recall how the skull was a key component in the ritual used by the Fox Maiden in her transformation from fox to maiden in conjunction with the invocations to the Big Dipper. The Big Dipper was considered in Daoist and Japanese thought to be the point where energies of creation are 'injected ' into material reality.

The skull becomes in itself a living being, a familiar if you will. We cannot help but point out that this practice is very widespread. In the Western Tradition for example, we have the tradition of the Oracular Head. This was a preserved head or skull that would 'speak' with the owner. In my own country, the head of Bran the Blessed was meant to have been buried on Tower Hill in London. Similar tales of oracular heads filtered through into popular culture ... Roger Bacon and his oafish assistant Friar Bungay were supposed to possess one, as was the Cornelius Agrippa, re-imagined in folklore. Several grimoires possess instructions for using skulls as the basis for experiments as familiar spirits and even invisibility.

The best kind of skull in Tachikawa was the skull made from a paste of the powdered tops of the skulls of a thousand men. The skull was said to resonate with the vibrations of the Po Soul of the long-gone owner. To explain this, in Daoist belief, every person had two basic souls. The Hun Soul and the Po Soul. The Hun Soul was the divine essence and higher parts of the individual. At death, this would pass on to whatever state existed beyond death. The Po Soul, however, often called the corporeal soul was the lower, earthly soul that remained on earth after death. It has a rudimentary intelligence and in magic is the basis of necromancy and other forms of so-called ghost magic.

It has a lot in common with western ideas of the astral shell in western occultism and theosophy.

In Chinese and Japanese occultism the Po Soul can be used as a basis for cultivating ghost magic. In its 'raw' form, the Po soul possesses varying degrees of intelligence and raw desire, feelings and so forth. By cultivating it in ritual processes the Po soul can be purified and grown to such a degree that it becomes extremely powerful as a familiar spirit. This is the basis of the Tachikawa Skull Ritual.

Once the magician obtained the skull it was placed on an altar. Over time he must create the face of a beautiful man or girl. He uses clay to build up a chin and flesh but adding layers of the combined male semen, vaginal fluids and menstrual blood. Occasionally he will lacquer it. He builds eyes from jewels etc according to his ingenium. Layers of gold and silver foil are incorporated into the skull, and cinnabar is used to colour the lips. Incense is burned in the skull. This should be frankincense, the incense of necromancy par excellence in Asian magic.

The skull is kept on the altar and fed daily with tea, rice and cooked eggs. Invocations are said by the master calling on the aid of the Fox Maiden.

In time the skull familiar will speak with the magician, at first in dreams and then in the reality of the practice home. Certain unspecified powers (siddhi) will arise.

What we learn from the Fox Fairy is the importance of the energies of sexuality and death in the immortalisation of the adept in Daoism.

In Daoist theory, alchemy is the transmutation of the adept into a being known as the Xian or Immortal. Immortal in Daoism means one who has created a new spiritual body by use of the imagination and will, in conjunction with various energies.

Many modern people assume that we have an astral body, an etheric body or soul that is capable of surviving the massive trauma of death, but this, according to Taoists, is wholly untrue. We may indeed have those spiritual forces and energies in a raw form but they are uncrystallised and unformed in the average person. By will and imagination, the Daoist crystallises and shapes those forces by interior alchemy into an immortal magical body that can even transcend death.

The forces of sexuality are one of the fundamental raw materials used as the basis of this transmutation. This is the Jing or 'Yellow' spoken of amongst the Fox maidens. In the legends of Kitsune, feeding on her lover's 'yellow' in Japanese lore, and the Chinese Hu Li Jing feeding upon the jing or essence/vigour of her victim, this sexual vampirism was fuel to her process of alchemical immortalisation.

As practitioners, we can utilise the sexual forces of our lovers to aid rather than hinder our occult development. This should be seen as a consensual and loving practice with both partners allowing and giving energy.

In Chinese tradition, this act should be between a man and a woman, Yin and Yang. Now I know that many in our own times may regret that this mystery seems to exclude an LGBT approach and that this cosmology does not reflect these rights in its expression of alchemy as taught by the ancient Fox Cult. I am not saying such a path does not exist, merely that I have not thus far found it in traditional Chinese alchemy, and I do not feel qualified to make this addition to the tradition. I must leave it to others to make such an adaptation.

A man possesses an abundance of Yang and a woman of Yin. In sexual alchemy, they can pass along their Yang or Yin energies to their partner *consciously* and use it to help build and 'fertilise' the inner magical body of immortality.

This can begin with a simple energy exchange such as the man and woman sitting in their usual meditation posture, palms held up to face or even touch. The couple then creates a circulation of energies. Pushing Yang energy from his dantain up his central channel and through the centre of his palms and into hers. She receives it and leads it into her dantian, then circulates it up through her spine and into his palms. They thus create a wheel of combined sexual energies.

When engaging in sexual, genital to genital alchemy the process is similar. As this is an incredibly complex subject this will be dealt with in another book in this series.

Another practice is of course sex with Huxian herself. This is often a process that occurs within the crossroads of waking and sleep. Another modality is when needing fuel for alchemy, one visualizes congress with the Fox Maiden. In men, this will lead to arousal of the sexual energies and erection but ejaculation will be avoided. Then the raw energies created by arousal are reversed inwards to be used for the growth of the magical body by way of the Dan Tian.

Essence Of The Moon And Sun

An important teaching in the Tantra of the Fox as a whole is the use of astral energies to empower and build the immortal body, or in more poetic terms to create the Pearl of Power.

In folklore, the ancient Chinese taught that the Fox Spirit would draw upon the powers of the Sun and especially the Moon by drinking of their essence to attain the state of an immortal being.

This is a well known Daoist practice. Qi-Gong means in a rough translation, the Art of Working with Qi. In Chinese thought, Qi is an omnipresent universal life force that all things are made of and sustained by. Its origin is in the Great Unknown Absolute referred to as Tian, Heaven.

In our solar system, Qi comes from the Sun but by the law of polarity is polarised by the Moon. Thus in the ancient Chinese language, the Sun is called Taiyang, the Great Yang and the Moon is called Taiyin, the Great Yin.

As Qi enters the zone of the Earth it reaches us in two major forms. The Yin and the Yang. The Moon in its roughly 28-day orbit around the Earth polarises some of it to be in a Yin essence form. While the Sun polarises it in its 24-hour cycle that comprises the day.

This teaching is yet, astonishingly, exactly reflected in the traditions of the West. It is often thought that one of the missing elements of the Western tradition is the idea of a universal energy that is somehow the medium of spiritual and magical force. This is simply not the case. For centuries it was a carefully guarded secret among the Hermeticists and alchemists. The famous Emerald Tablet in my opinion speaks about it plainly to those with ears to listen:

> And as all things have been and arose from one by the mediation of one: so all things have their birth from this one thing by adaptation.
> The Sun is its father, the moon its mother,
> the wind hath carried it in its belly, the earth is its nurse.
> The father of all perfection in the whole world is here.
> Its force or power is entire if it is converted into earth.
> Separate thou the earth from the fire,
> the subtle from the gross
> sweetly with great industry.

It ascends from the earth to the heaven and again it
descends to the earth
and receives the force of things superior and inferior.
By this means you shall have the glory of the whole
world and thereby all obscurity shall fly from you.
Its force is above all force,
for it vanquishes every subtle thing and penetrates every
solid thing.
So was the world created.
From this are and do come admirable adaptations
whereof the means is here in this.
Hence I am called Hermes Trismegistus, having the
three parts of the philosophy of the whole world.
That which I have said of the operation of the Sun is
accomplished and ended.

This is the same model as for Qi in Daoism, Prana in Yoga
and the Astral Light/Magnetic-Electric Fluid in western magic.

'The wind carries it in its belly' is a reference to the idea
that the universal spirit is linked to the air we breathe. The primary
source for Qi is via the breath, the 'wind'. Atmospheric air is
somehow mysteriously charged with the universal life force. It
exists in two main forms: Solar or Yang and Lunar or Yin.

The master of western magic will call these electrical (yang)
and magnetical (yin). Furthermore, a master can separate the
two and use them for different functions, or in combination for
various effects.

Returning to the mysterious process said to have been
enjoyed by the Foxes which was the imbibing of these energies.
Once you know how, the process is simple but the mastery is
hard!

As another interesting sideline, the Witches of Thessaly in
ancient Greece were said to have mastered a technique known
as Drawing Down the Moon in order to fuel their sorcery and,

yes, transformations into animals and the like ... another parallel with the Fox tradition.

The ancient scriptures of Maoshan also teach how to draw in the Essence of the Moon.

The most common method is to physically look at the moon, standing in a relaxed posture and gazing at it. Some texts suggest protruding the tongue. Breathe in the essence of the Moon and visualise its yellow light building on the tip of the tongue in a bubble. When you intuitively feel it is ready, swallow and nestle it in the Dantian. Practice regularly at least weekly.

One can also practice without the Moon being present, simply visualising the Moon above the crown point of the top of your head. With natural breathing. Inhale the yellow lunar 'cream' down your central channel into the dantian.

More complex methods are to capture the lunar essence in water or talismans or a combination of the two and drink the lunar essence, storing it in the dantian.

The method of imbibing the solar essence is almost identical. The magician simply faces the Sun. Ideally, this would be done on waking and facing the East as the solar disc is rising. Breathing in the red energy and storing it in the dantian to add to the total store of Qi.

The Fox Glamour

This spell is popular with those who need a glamorous charisma. It is frequently used by entertainers, singers, actors and even public speakers as well as sex workers, to draw in more customers.

The ritual again is simple. The practitioner sets up a simple altar with red candles and an image of the Nine Tail Fox. It is highly recommended, if at all possible, that on the altar is a real fox fur, white if possible. The incense to be burned is Hu Xian's favourite, agarwood. Yang incense such as sandalwood can never be used.

It is also recommended that the disciple offers fresh flowers and the kind of items you would buy a girlfriend: perfume, makeup, lipstick and so on.

Each night, but especially at full moon time, the devotee sits before the altar of the fox and lays his or her hand on the fox fur.

The practitioner must now mentally visualise the Fox Lady. This should not be merely an internal image in the mind. Have your eyes half open and visualise her before you, OUTSIDE of you as a real presence in the space before you. See her in a three-dimensional form. With time the visualised Fox Maiden will become more stable and more real. At the end of each visualisation session, you should absorb that image into yourself, superimpose it if you like. See her ability to make you more charming pour into you.

At the end of the session thank the Fox Maiden with three bows. Now according to the Chinese not only will you seem more charismatic, but there will also be subtle physical changes. A sure sign of success is said to be a subtle shift in the shape of the eyes which take on an upward slanting shape similar to the Asian Fox. This is one of the more extreme effects reported by the Chinese and I am not saying it will happen, but there is the warning as supplied by tradition!

Fox Talismans

Central to the practice of Taoist magic is the use of Fu talismans. Fu talismans are written commands that capture the essence of not only the will of the magician but of the very forces he evokes.

At first glance, Taoist talismans look very exotic and strange to westerners accustomed to seeing say Qabalistic or Solomonic variety. However, they are not so different.

Even the processes are remarkably similar to those of the Key of Solomon.

The tools needed to write talismans include yellow paper, a Chinese style brush pen, an inkstone for grinding ink and an ink block. Normally a small porcelain dish with a little ladle is also prepared.

These four main items, the pen, paper, ink and inkstone are known as the Four Treasures of Study. Each of these is consecrated for use and, yes, just like the western tradition all the items must be 'virgin', that is previously unused for any other purpose.

The subject of creating consecrating talismans will be fully and copiously uncovered in a companion volume in this Chinese magic series, however, for the sake of completeness, I will give the reader, who is likely gasping to try Fox Magic, a quick rundown.

Now talisman writing will require a quiet room where the Taoist mage will not be disturbed. You will have an altar which can also be the fox shrine. However, this altar should be clear enough to enable you to write on it.

At a minimum, you need two red candles set in candlesticks, an incense burner and an image of Huxian. You can also use the Fox Temple Power Chart or Fairy Chart as it is sometimes called.

The Fairy Chart serves a function somewhat like an Enochian Tablet in the Western Tradition. It details the names of the Spirits sacred to the Daoist Magical Tradition and secondly, serves as a battery and engine of magical power for the altar.

Ideally, you will want the Altar in the Northern Quarter of the room. Now on the Altar have prepared the Four Treasures, i.e., the Pen, the Paper, the Ink and the Inkstone.

The pen is the Chinese brush. You should have two of them. One for black ink, which is stored in a black cloth. Another for red ink which is stored in a red cloth.

The paper as mentioned before should be yellow rice paper which has been especially dyed and made for Daoist talismans. This can easily be bought online. It is important if you intend to burn or even eat the ashes of talismans that it is made of edible materials.

The ink should be good ink sold in sticks. If possible do not buy prepared liquid ink. Part of the ritual process involves grinding the ink and so, obviously, if it is liquid you miss part of the ritual process. The grinding of the ink has an important empowering function. You will need a black stick, which is usually made of pine soot and other gums and herbs.

The red ink is for more specialized talismans. Red ink needs some caution as it contains cinnabar. However, this ink has a powerful virtue in Chinese magic that we just cannot ignore. If you write talismans for carrying, or for placing on your altar there is no real harm.

You will need an inkstone. This is usually a circular or oblong trough of slightly rough stone with a grain that allows you to grind ink into a powder. The magician will add a little consecrated water to the inkstone and grind. The powder will suspend itself in the water. When it is a satisfactory depth of colour the ink is ready for use.

Finally, you will need a small ceramic dish to hold water. Have all the items arranged on the table.

Cleanliness is of great importance, so generally, it is

recommended to have a bath or shower and clean your teeth before conducting the ritual. The time chosen will be between 11 pm and 1 am the so-called Zi Hour. This is the liminal hour of Chinese philosophy where the Yin and Yang forces are at near-perfect balance. It is an extremely magical time and full of liminal power.

First, you must step the Big Dipper Pattern to call upon the powers of the Heavens. As we mentioned earlier, the Big Dipper is a major source of power in the Taoist tradition. The Big Dipper Step hearkens back to the earliest days of Chinese magic and was said to originate with the great Shaman-King Yu the Great. I have attached this method in the cheat sheets in this volume.

Once the magician has stepped the Big Dipper, thus invoking the powers of the Heavens and their mysteries, he or she can consecrate the Pen, the Water, the Ink and the Paper.

1. The Paper Spell

O Northern Emperor strike this and command this paper to exorcise these unhealthy spirits and send them to the Underworld!! (Fengdu) Ji Ji Ru Lu Ling!!

2. The Ink Spell

O Jade Emperor, this ink is magical ink, I see a blazing mist from the Nine Star God above it, grinding the ink with power like a thunderbolt vajra striking!!
Ji Ji Ru Luling.

3. The Pen Spell

The Five Thunder Gods descend, sending lightning, burning brilliantly, and receiving here to cause evil ghosts to disintegrate, the ghost road is closed. I am long-lived!!
Ji Ji Ru Luling!!

4. The Spell To Be Said When Grinding The Ink In The Inkstone

O Jade Emperor grinding this ink, the God looks upon the Four Directions, Metal, Wood, Water, Fire and Earth, Thunder, Wind, Rain and Lightning, the Gods grind the ink, the electrical flash of the thunderbolt is boundless!!

Ji Ji Ru Lu Ling!!

5. The Water Spell

This here is not ordinary water, it is extraordinary water, the Northern Power, the Ren-Gui Water, the clouds and rain. The sick drink it and they are healed, a hundred ghosts disappear, guarding against evil, ghosts disintegrate!!

Ji Ji Ru Luling!!

When all this is accomplished the scholar can grind the ink ready for use. He or she can now offer prayers and perhaps make a statement as to his or her intent in writing the talisman. Now the magus can write the talisman itself. Please refer to the cheat sheets on how to do this.

Once the magician has finished writing the talisman. Use the Sword Finger Mudra and point to the talisman and stamp your left foot.

Finally circle the talisman through the incense smoke three, seven or nine times. The talisman is now ready for use.

Next follows several Fox Talisman designs. Some are very famous in China and Asia for their power. Many of them are associated with the power of love, charisma and sexuality.

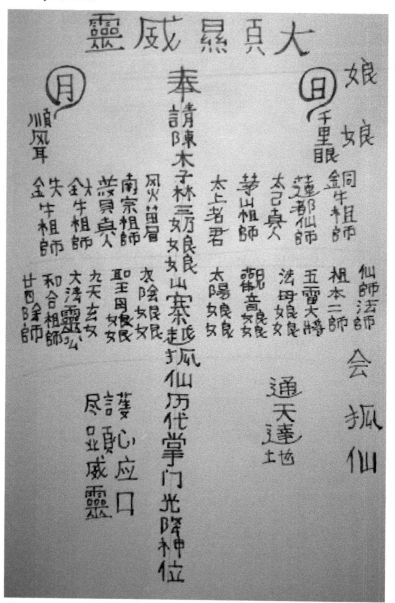

Power Tablet Design For The Altar

TALISMAN STRUCTURE.

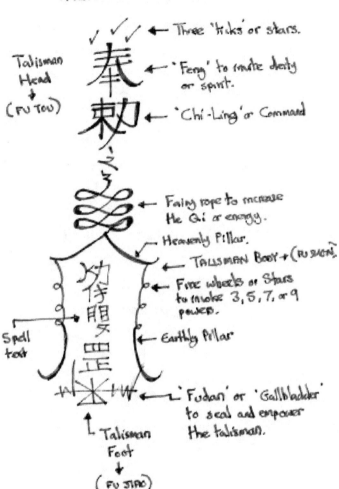

Three 'ticks' or stars.

Talisman Head
↓
(FU TOU)

'Feng' to invite deity or spirit.

'Chi-Ling' or Command

Fairy rope to increase the Qi or energy.

Heavenly Pillar.

TALISMAN BODY → (FU SHEN)

Five wheels or Stars to invoke 3, 5, 7, or 9 powers.

Earthly Pillar

Spell text

'Fudan' or 'Gallbladder' to seal and empower the talisman.

Talisman Foot
↓
(FU JIAO)

Talisman Cheat Sheet 1

符頭 = Fu Tou = Talisman Head.

1. The Futou or talisman head at the top is the first thing drawn.

2. These were originally three points, but evolved into three 'tick' marks due to the nature of the Chinese brush.

3. Most often they represent the San Qing, the 'Three Pure Ones', the highest triad of Daoist theology.

4. With each cheek or 'dian' (point) recite the spell.

① To Dianzun Tianshang Laojun.
② To Yuanshi Tianzun.
③ To Lingbao Tianzun.

The San Qing.

5.

② ① ③

INVOCATION

66 " Yi bi, Tian xia dong Zhongjian ! (✓) ①
" Er bi, Zushi Jian ! (✓) ②
" San bi, Xiong shen (✓) ③
" È sha qu qian li ! " (Sword fingers) 99

"One stroke, the universe trembles!
Second stroke, the Ancestral Sword strikes! "
Third stroke and the evil ghosts flee a
thousand miles!"

☆ On completion "stab" three points with
Sword Seal to watch them flare up with light.

Talisman Cheat Sheet 2

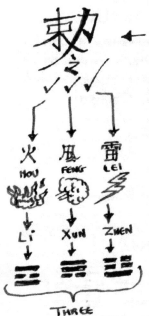

火
HOU

风
FENG

雷
LEI

↓
Li

↓
XUN

↓
ZHEN

THREE
MOVING POWERS
of
Nature or
the THREE GENERALS
(SAN JIANGJUN)

← The 'san dian' or Three Points
are underneath the 'Chi-Ling'
or 'Command Character', it
is NOT San Qing, but is
Thunder, Wind and Fire.
Sometimes they are given
as :

②①③

This form is used in more
forceful spells, or spells
requiring gathering more
elemental power.
On each stroke simply
say "Feng" – Wind
"Hou" – Fire
"Lei !" – Thunder !

Visualise and invoke each
power. For example, breathe
in RED FIRE Qi, visualising
a red mist extending to
the horizon and the Li
Trigram. Inhale to dan tian
and project through brush.

Another form is that of the San Guan or Three Officials or Three Monarchs, Powers etc. This form of the Three Points is called San Tai. The San Tai form is also always beneath the Command Character or Chi-ling.

东力 ← chi-ling.

← San Tai form.

2 3

The Three Officials very high deities directly under the Jade Emperor, they are:

天宫 Tianguan = Heaven	☰ QIAN
地宫 Diguan = Earth	☷ KUN
水宫 Shuiguan = WATER	☵ KAN

In writing the San Tai Spell is uttered as visualising and invoking them :

"SAN TAI SHENG WO, ✓1.
SAN TAI YANG WO ✓2
SAN TAI HU WO ! ✓3"

SAN TAI CREATES ME,
SAN TAI NOURISHES ME,
SAN TAI PROTECTS ME !

Talisman Cheat Sheet 4

CHI-LING

1. Chi-Ling or "Fu-Ling" essentially means "to command" or to give an order.

2. It is composed of the characters:

束 又令

In the Chinese language it is suggestive of an "Imperial Edict" or "Military Command" of a general and it is in this feeling it should be written with absolute conviction.

3. The 'Ling' part or 令 is often incorporated into the talisman design, usually the horizontal "Heavenly Pillar" so as to encompass the written intention of the spell.

4. Designs that can be used:

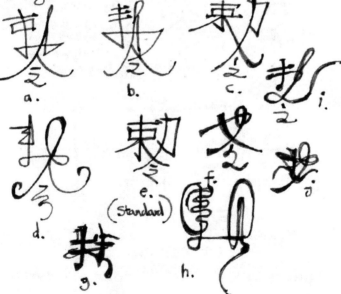

a.　b.　c.　i.

d.　e. (Standard)　f.　j.

g.　h.

TALISMANS (四)

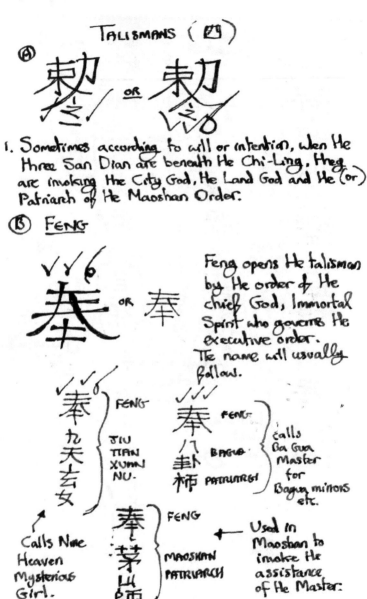

(A)

1. Sometimes according to will or intention, when the three San Dian are beneath the Chi-Ling, they are invoking the City God, the Land God and the (or) Patriarch of the Maoshan Order.

(B) FENG

Feng opens the talisman by the order of the chief God, Immortal Spirit who governs the executive order.
The name will usually follow.

FENG
JIU TIAN XUAN NU.

Calls Nine Heaven Mysterious Girl.

FENG
BAGUA
PATRIARCH
Calls Ba Gua Master for Bagua mirrors etc.

FENG
MAOSHAN PATRIARCH
Used in Maoshan to invoke the assistance of the Master.

Talisman Cheat Sheet 6.

FUDAN or GALLBLADDER.

1. A talisman is a living vessel of power. The Fudan 'locks the door' of the talisman to prevent energy leaking out and undesirable energy entering.

2. The Spell Formula for the Fudan is as follows. Remember this is done last.

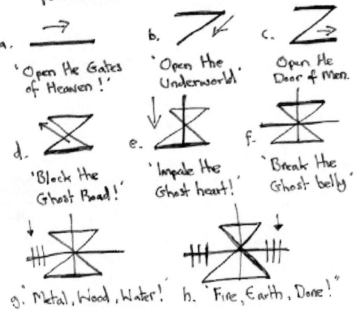

a. 'Open the Gates of Heaven!'

b. 'Open the Underworld'.

c. Open the Door of Men.

d. 'Block the Ghost Road!'

e. 'Impale the Ghost heart!'

f. 'Break the Ghost belly'

g. 'Metal, Wood, Water!'

h. 'Fire, Earth, Done!'

Talisman Cheat Sheet 7.
The gallbladder sigil is drawn to finalise the talisman. With each stroke of the pen say the spell.

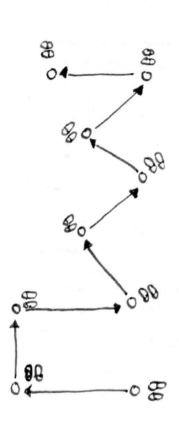

Seven-Star Steps for Talisman Making.

* Left foot goes first, then drag right foot next to left. The 'dragging' foot slides on the ground.

* Mudra is right Sword Finger with index and middle fingers grasped by the left fist.

Stepping the Seven Stars, step by step, Ascending the Heavens, The Three Wonders - Sun, Moon and Stars, Heaven is with me, the Twenty-Eight Stars too. Jiu Tian Xuan Nu Comes!
  Ji Ji Ru Luling!

Talisman Cheat Sheet 8.
Big Dipper Stepping Pattern to be used in consecrating talismans.

Nine Tail Fox Altar Image

1. The Mountain Fox helps in prosperity and fortune.

Fox Talisman For Prosperity And Fortune. It Also Aids In Meeting the Right People And Being Popular Socially.

The Fox Soul Hook Used To Fascinate, Seduce And Bewitch. It Should Be Carried Or Drawn On The Palm.

Immortal
Whore
Immortal
Teacher
Induces
Passion.

A Powerful Charm Sacred To The Fox As The Holy Harlot For Inducing Intense Sexual Passion.

Female
Poisons
Man to
Passion.

(Nu Gu nan Ganging)

Powerful Talisman Of Sorcerous Female Ku. Causes Bewitchment And Erotic Passion. Ku Or Gu Is An Ancient Form Of Witchcraft Using Animal Potencies To Project Yin Forces.

Bewitchment And Fascination Charm Used To Enchant The Soul Of The Target. It Is Drawn On Yellow Paper And Reduced To Ashes. Let The beloved Come Into Contact With Powder. Or Draw On Your Palm And Touch Them. Or Carry The Charm.

Carry This To Have The Glamour Of The Fox. You will be Fascinating.
Specifically it will attract the opposite sex.

To break an
unhealthy
love or
obsession.

Stop Love Or Bewitchment. To Rid Of A Love Or Obsession.

Brother Pig and Fox Power of Joining Male and Female.

For Love Magic Or Healing A Marriage That Is Vexed.

The Fox Seizes Love.
(Huli duo Qingyuan)

The Fox Seizes Love. Psychic Seduction Talisman.

Fox Shrine In A Uk Temple. Note
The So Called Fairy Chart And Fox Skin.

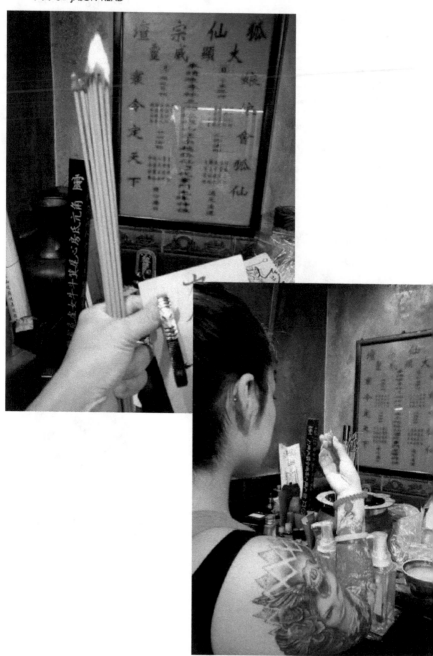

Fox Temple In Hong Kong.

Hu Xian In Statue Form.

Immortal Fox Girl Statue Undergoes Kai Guang To 'enliven' The Statue. The Brush Has Cinnabar That Is Used To 'point' The Five Senses Of The Image.

Incense Offerings To Lady Hu. Incense Is The Key Ingredient To Set Up A
Viable And Reciprocal Relationship Between The Devotee And The Gods.

Maoshan Seizes Love Skill

What now follows is an example of Chinese magic for love. The author warns that this is a somewhat unethical technique by today's standards, but is very powerful. Caution is recommended. It was used by the Maoshan school of magic to seize love, DUO AI.

The sorcerer would first obtain the name and the date of birth of the target. Ideally this is the year, month and day. The so-called Eight Characters, because the date of birth in Chinese can be rendered into eight characters or Ba Zi in Chinese.

The magician obtains a blue and white porcelain bowl. A *catty* measure (600g) of dried white rice.

With red paper he cuts out two figures, one male and one female. And he also has an ivory or bone needle.

Taking up the red paper doll he draws on them the five sensory organs or wu guan, and dots them with cinnabar as he envisions light and life causing them to be real living beings. He writes the names and birthdates of the couple over the hearts of the paper dolls.

He pours the white rice into the bowl and sets the paper doll representing the target in the bowl.

He now steps the Big Dipper and inhales Qi from the East and blows onto the paper doll, and then quickly takes a Soul Stirring Talisman (She Hun Fu) and burns it above the red paper doll moving it in three or seven circles above it as the talisman burns.

With the ivory needle he stabs it vertically into the heart of the paper doll, stares at the doll and chants:

Heaven seeks and Earth seeks, undertake to chase
.... name of target .... And swiftly assist ....

name of client ...., the Three Spirits and Seven
Souls come together, merging into one heart, they join
as one, the method of attracting harmony to make the
two beauties one.

Ji ji ru lu ling!!

As he or she chants the spell the needle is twisted. This
operation is done for seven consecutive days.

On the seventh day, the magician takes the client's doll and
binds them face to face with red thread. Bind them at the waist
in 49 circles and tie a final knot.

The warlock now holds his left hand in thunder mudra (a
fist) and inserts his index and middle fingers of his right hand
(sword mudra). He holds the paper dolls over incense smoke
and chants:

Heaven wonders, Earth wonders, the secret method
to pursue the heart and join them as one heart...come,
come, come and chase .... name ...... on behalf of
...... name ......, join them, respond, join the two
without them knowing!!

Ji ji Ru Luling.

To finish, the sorcerer puts the bound dolls into a lidded
porcelain jar.

Repeat the operation from 7 to 49 days.

When finally successful the dolls are buried beneath a tree.

Overleaf is the Stir the Soul Talisman.

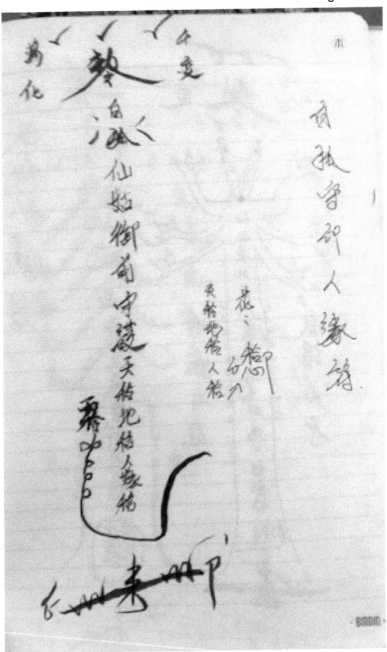

Copy of original Fox Temple manuscript

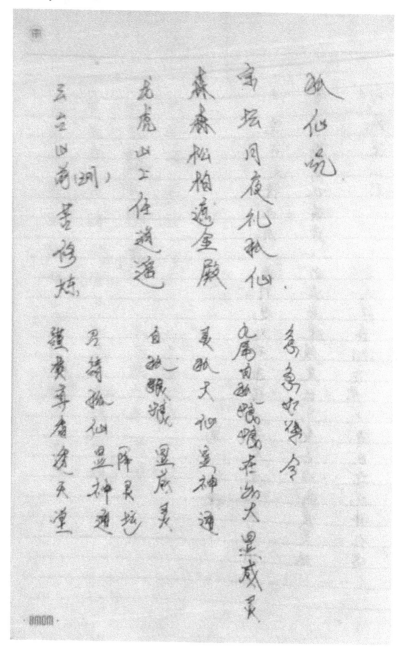

Copy of Fox Temple Manuscript. An invocation of the Fox

GLOSSARY

BEI MA: A cult in North Eastern China whose principle method of magic and worship is devotion to certain nature spirits who often manifest themselves through mediumship. These include the python, snake, weasel, bird , bear, tiger and ghost.

CHAKRAS: Literally 'wheels' in Sanskrit. Are centres of experience within the occult anatomy as envisioned by Tantric science.

BODHISATTVA: In Buddhist thought a saint who has spurned complete nirvana in order to serve and lead life into enlightenment.

DIAMOND VAJRA REALM: The realm of archetypal spirit, the Heavenly Realm in Shingon and Mikkyo esoteric thought. It is symbolised by masculine and Yang imagery. The Diamond thunderbolt is certainly phallic in its implication and penetrates the WOMB REALM to manifest the archetypal ideas into actuality. It can also be seen as pure consciousness.

DAKINI: A female spirit originating in Indian lore. In certain yogic practices dakinis were often invoked to work with the yogi, sometimes sexually, to obtain occult powers and knowledge. The practice was incorporated by Buddhism.

DAKINITEN: Japanese goddess who originated from the Himalayan gnosis. She is depicted riding a white fox.

DIZI: Chinese term for a disciple and practitioner of Taoism.

DOUBLE CULTIVATION: The art of sexual qigong in which the couple , using visualisation and breath control to circulate and strengthen internal energies to build the magical body of immortality.

EROS: The principle of sexuality both in the biosphere and the cosmos. It is symbolised by the colour red in asian magic.

FIVE ELEMENTS: The five elements come in two forms.
In the chinese system they are Wood, Metal, Fire, Soil and Water. The Tantric systems introduced via Buddhism are Akasha, Air, Fire, Water and Earth.

FIVE ORGANS: The five internal organs are the solid organs within the human body. They are considered to be direct manifestations of the five Chinese elements. Much work in the early stages of chinese magic is devoted to internally communicating with these organs and their spirits. They are the heart, the kidneys, the spleen, the liver and the gallbladder.

GNOSIS: Occult knowledge obtained by experience and practice in contrast to faith or pistis. The ancient and universal symbol of this knowledge has long been the serpent and dragon. A Sanskrit cognate is JNANA.

GOLDEN LIGHT PRACTICE: One of the most important exercises in magical Daoism is to invoke and create a magical body by congealing and crystallising the golden essence of solar particles said to be in our atmosphere.

GU: An ancient form of Chinese sorcery using the power of Yin. At its most basic it was the art of using yin poisons derived from insects, centipedes, serpents and toads to enchant, curse or control the mind of the target. At a more gnostic level gu was non physical and involved the use of yin spirits as familiars. Kenneth Grant mentions this practice in his works.

HU LI JING: The most frequent term for fox spirit in Chinese.

HUN: The higher causal soul in man. At death it is the Hun Soul that is the essence that survives post-mortem trauma.

HU XIAN: The Fox Immortal. One of the highest forms of the fox spirit who by yoga and cultivation has achieved divinity and immortality.

INARI: Japanese form of the Fox Goddess associated with fertility, rice, sake and the art of the blacksmith.

JI JI RU LU LING: A chinese term at the end of spells. It can be translated as QUICKLY BY COMMAND and in essence has the same meaning as So Mote it Be. It has its own mantric power and seals and actualises a spell.

JING: Raw and unrefined sexual force. This forms the basis of transmutations in the workings of occult inner alchemy.

KITSUNE: Japanese term for Hu Li Jing, a fox spirit.

KUNLUN: A mythical mountain that is the cosmic axis in Chinese symbolism. It is the equivalent of the Indian and Tibetan Mount Meru. In the body Mount Kunlun is the spine.

KU: See gu.

LUBAN: In ancient times a well known engineer and carpenter in old China now revered in Feng Shui and magical circles. Many old texts supposedly written by Luban are grimoires of chinese magic.

MI HUN: In chinese, to bewitch, fascinate or overshadow, control the soul of a person. In modern Chinese it can be rendered as ecstasy and hypnotism.

NEI GONG: Inner Work, the chinese term for inner occult alchemy. The goal is longevity and health initially, but ultimately a kind of immortality that transcends space and time.

ONMYODO: A Japanese esoteric art meaning the Way of Yin and Yang. Primarily it analyses the Yin and Yang of any situation and offers various magical solutions.

PEARL: In Chinese and Japanese occultism is a coagulated and condensed manifestation of spiritual power. The idea is similar to the Philosopher's Stone of western alchemy.

PO: The lower soul or mortal soul in man is in charge of lower functions and desires. It is directly comparable to the lower astral body or astral shell of theosophy. It is believed to survive death for a number of years and manifest as a ghost. It is also the basis for certain lower forms of magical necromancy.

POST HEAVEN: Chinese term for the state of being in physical existence. In Chinese thought we begin the process of losing our jing, sexo-spiritual essence and the inevitable decay begins.

PRE HEAVEN: The state of incorruptibility before birth into the physical world. The spiritual state.

QI: Universal energy that permeates and penetrates all things. All created things contain and are made of it.

SAN QING: The Three Pure Ones. The highest deities of Taoism who manifest and order the universe as well as project the essence of spiritual wisdom into the Land Under Heaven that all living beings may find a spiritual path.

SHEN: The higher spiritual energy in man.

SHINTO: Japanese religion of nature spirits or kami, is very similar to Daoism in many respects and in fact derives from Shen Dao, the Chinese Way of the Gods.

SIDDHI: Sanskrit term for occult or magical powers.

SWORD MUDRA: Most popular hand seal in Japanese and Chinese magic represents a spiritual sword. The index and middle fingers are extended to form the blade.

TAISHANG LAOJUN: The spiritual and magical form of the philosopher Lao Zu. In Daoist magic Taishang has manifested as a spiritual teacher on earth many times, only one form being Lao Zu, author of the Tao te Ching. He is in charge of the evolution and spiritual progression of mankind.

TAIYANG: The Sun and the solar yang essence.

TAIYIN: The Moon and the lunar yin essence.

THANATOS: Term for mysteries of death. In asian culture it is symbolised by the colour white.

TUDI: The spirit of a place.

WOMB REALM: The earthly realm of experience and effect.

YELLOW: Term for jing or sexual essence in Japanese tantra.

ZHANG DAOLING: The spiritual founder of magical Daoism known also as the Celestial Master. He is depicted riding on a tiger, a symbol of the conquest and mastery of matter.

Index

Printed in the USA
CPSIA information can be obtained
at www.ICGtesting.com
LVHW020906260923
759107LV00019B/1112